The Creative C.O.R.E. Method

A Practical People's Guide to Creativity for Personal Transformation

VIVIAN GEFFEN

RITZ
BOOKS

The Creative C.O.R.E. Method:
A Practical People's Guide to Creativity for Personal Transformation

Copyright © 2024 Vivian Geffen
Paperback ISBN: 978-1-960460-19-6
Kindle ISBN: 978-1-960460-20-2

Published by RITZ BOOKS
Cover design & interior layout by Steph Ritz

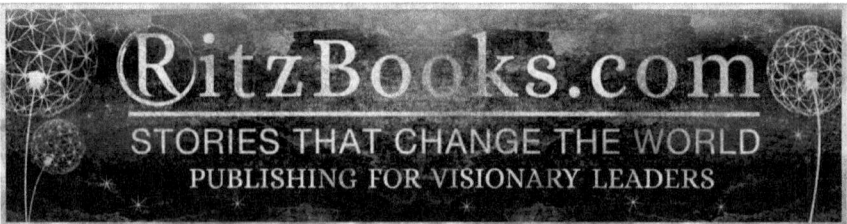

RitzBooks.com
STORIES THAT CHANGE THE WORLD
PUBLISHING FOR VISIONARY LEADERS

Dedication

To the child inside the adult who always wanted to know
they were creative and be acknowledged for it.

You are!

And we see you now.

Note to the Reader

Table of Contents

An Introduction to Flexible Thinking

When I truly realized that I could be creative without ever worrying about being good at art, it was an enormous relief. I was freed from a misconception and realized that creative expression could be explored in many other ways.

I had always been drawn to the realm of personal transformation; I was a seeker and workshop enthusiast all my adult life. But each experience, although healing and fun, never really addressed the core pain I felt... that I was not able to find a means to be recognized as creative in the way I came to believe that people are creative.

I believed that being good at art was the only way to be recognized as being creative. Therefore, even though I felt that I had something unique to share, I did not see how I could express it or manifest it given my lack of artistic abilities. This led to years of feeling invisible and unempowered. Sometime in my thirties, I was talking to a coach and blurted out that I wanted to be a

"Creativity Muse." I was embarrassed as soon as the words came out because my immediate thoughts were: Who am I? How can I? What does it even mean?

In spite of the doubt, deep inside the words felt true they were my call to action. It took time for the form and meaning to coalesce because I had to get the tools, build confidence, and mature into it. The big "a-ha" moment for me was figuring out how creativity could be used as a tool for transformation. Once I latched onto that perspective, the vision opened up. I knew how I could embody the expression of being the Creativity Muse. This book is a part of that expression, because I want to reach as many as possible with this empowering message about creativity.

If you are looking for ways to express your creativity and desire to make changes in yourself and your life, all you need to do to get started is open yourself to the possibility.

Get ready to engage mindsets of curiosity and openness. Orient yourself towards making interesting connections and set yourself on a course of action.

Whether you want to change some of the foundational pieces of your life (like career track), or be better in your relationships, the attributes of the creative mindset will serve you. When you develop awareness of the natural rhythm of the creative process, you can be mindful, intentional, and kind to yourself as you create change internally and externally.

My hope is that you get to the end of this book and feel empowered, transformed, and courageous as you move towards your heart's desire.

Part 1:

What's Possible?

Redefining Creativity

Chapter 1:

Who Am I to be Creative?

Have you ever had the experience of singing along with a song for years, maybe decades, and then one day someone looks at you funny and says, "Those aren't the words." In a moment of blinding clarity, you realize you've been hearing and singing it wrong for years, maybe even decades? When it is a song, the experience can be quite funny and inconsequential. However, what happens when it is a misinterpretation that came from a person you looked up to, like a parent or teacher?

An off-handed comment, spoken in passing that you internalized and held as true, can become a foundational belief you build your life upon. One day, something happens that shakes that idea free and you see it for what it is. When that happens, and you recognize that it's not true, it can feel shattering and not so funny.

In a heartbeat, you might see that those beliefs impacted your choices and the roads you took, for better or worse.

A misunderstanding of that magnitude is what happened to me and my relationship with creativity. It took me until middle age to reinterpret, rearrange, and relaunch onto a new creatively inspired path. In this book I share my story, the remedy (in the form of the tools I have learned), and a vision for you: to discard those misunderstandings or beliefs that impacted you. You too can embrace and embody your desires; how you want to be seen, known and interacted with; and what you want to contribute while on this planet.

How it all started

I was eight years old when I arrived home from school one afternoon and, after dropping my Scooby-Doo lunchbox on the round, oak kitchen table, noticed a small, square colorful newspaper. On the cover was my favorite singer, Cher, and to my surprise, beside her stood my uncle. I picked it up and read that they were dating. In my little eight-year-old brain, fireworks started going off. This was exciting! Were they going to get married? Was I going to meet her? Was she going to become my aunt? Would she come to my house? How did my uncle even know this TV star? Wasn't she married to Sonny?

Dad would know. I waited impatiently for him to come home from work. When he did, I showed him the paper and asked if Cher was going to be my aunt.

Without a pause he said no. I wondered how he met her; he told me through work.

"What does Uncle do for work?" I asked.

He paused for a moment, thinking, and then said, "He discovers talent."

"Oh," I said, and walked away contemplating what "discovers talent" meant. To me, at that age, it meant that everyone had talent, and someone would come along (almost like a fairy godmother), tap you with their wand, and tell you what your talent was. Once you knew your talent, you would do that thing and naturally be good at it. Money and recognition would follow. The answer to that question adults always liked to ask, "What do you want to be when you grow up?" would be easily resolved once I had the answer.

I felt an enormous sense of excitement and anticipation wondering when and where my talent would be revealed. The wait was just beginning.

Hey Ma, look at me

In 1978 my family lived in Ladera Heights, California. It was a pretty, suburban neighborhood with mostly one-story 1970s houses and families with lots of kids. My best friend and I would walk to one another's home., There were kids on bikes throwing rocks or playing hopscotch on the sidewalk. Schools were being integrated at the time, so I was bussed to another school for 1st-3rd grades while the 4th-6th grades were all combined and went to the school down the street from me. In elementary school, we all got along fine. It didn't seem like a big deal. My teachers were nice and I was smart enough to learn to read and write. But things changed when my best friend got pulled into a "gifted" class and I didn't. I was jealous and didn't understand why she got to go to a special class and I didn't. Surely, I was as smart as she was. This felt like a real slap in the face for my ambitions of being discovered. My home life was not much more promising.

I have a sister; she is three years younger than me. We have always been close; I was never a sibling that didn't like my younger sister. We loved horses. We we played with our model horses and, with our supplies of paper, pencils and model horses spread out on the kitchen table, we would draw them. I would concentrate as hard as I could, following the outline of the horse, trying to translate it onto my paper. Somehow it always ended up looking like a fat, misshapen dog. "Ugh!" I would growl, upset, and discouraged. I would pound my fist onto the table, throw my pencil down and declare, "I can't draw!" Looking over at my sister's drawing, I would see a horse that looked like a horse. Clearly, she could draw. I felt a sense of envy, ire and distance. She had access to an ability that I did not. It was one little brick in the "less than" wall. Even at that age, I could see that access to creativity and talent was an empowering source of respect. I trudged on trying to find my special magic.

My sister, my mom, and I played music from an album by a French singer named Michele Polnareff. The cover had headphones and a big tongue that looked like a heart. We danced to a bouncy rock song called "Come on Lady Blue" and I just loved it; we took turns dancing and watching each other dance. I felt really into it, I was loose and wavy. I found a movement with my arm waving overhead that felt very good, almost dramatic, and my sister started to laugh and mock me. Instead of earning the praise I felt I deserved for how good that performance felt, I was laughed at and it hurt my feelings. My mom did not come to my defense and my imagined dancing prowess was not celebrated. It felt like yet another thing that I did to express myself was not appreciated. Check another option off the "talent I get discovered for" list.

A sense of desperation set in. I tried various activities hoping to be noticed, to be told this is where I can excel. Instead, it was just one rejection after the other.

I tried out for the school chorus. We had to take turns one at a time going up and singing in front of the room and the other students. I was so nervous. I loved to sing at home but had never sung in front of strangers before. But there I went, scared, vulnerable and intimidated. I did not get invited to sing in the chorus. That broke my heart. Yet another nail in the coffin of my sense of value. But it went on. There were ballet classes, tap classes, and ice-skating classes and in all of them I was given the message that I was not good enough.

There was no future (and fame and fortune) for me in any of those activities I tried.

By 5th grade I had exhausted my best ideas for getting discovered. A deep sadness took hold of me. I came to the devastating realization that I was not creative or talented enough to get discovered. The future felt bleak.

My little heart was broken and though I smiled on the outside, had friends and went through the world, there was a helplessness, a grief so deep that it influenced everything and made the experience of just being in my body almost unbearable. I began to see the world through a lens of comparison. Greater than or less than and I was always on the less than side. Instead of investing my time and energy developing a skill, I invested in self-judgment, picking up society's cues about the size of my body, and the value I had (or didn't have) because I was a chubby kid. I engaged in the associated addictive behaviors of overeating, and, eventually as a teenager and young adult, I developed an eating disorder.

Looking back, I realize that nobody took the time to tell me about practice and improvement. Since I had this idea that talent equaled "good at," I thought it meant that someone was good right out of the gate. From the adult perspective, I now know that learning anything takes time and practice. The old saying "anything worth doing well is worth doing badly" makes sense. Another layer in my misinterpretation came from the fact that I was growing up in Los Angeles around people who were involved with show business, and the message about that business was all about talent. Being good and being recognized – that was what made one important. There was some sense that the creative people were valued and desired, and I wasn't one of them.

Since I had concluded that I was not talented, I figured that meant I was not creative and, therefore, not valuable. I interpreted that as not being good enough in any way, shape or form. Had I been a different personality type, maybe I would have fought back and proved them wrong. I just thought adults knew what was up and took them at their word, especially when it came to me.

I was so shut down and believed my own narrative so strongly, that when people tried to compliment me or call me creative, I thought they were wrong; I was incapable of taking it to heart and feeling encouraged by their words.

Later, as I was healing from these misconceptions and finding my creativity, I remembered drawing those horses with my sister:

In retrospect that I would try once, twice, maybe three times and when I didn't see improvement I quit. I decided I couldn't draw and walked away. What I remembered was that she stayed, she erased, started over and worked at it. I don't remember what her horses looked like at first, but they became very good. I never recognized the time she put into her ability to be good. When I realized this, it was a lightbulb moment and my perceptions started to shift. I understood I had missed a few important life lessons.

The first lesson I missed was patience. The second was persistence.

Patience for process and the real work of improving over time

It takes persistence to navigate the gap between what your mind sees is possible, versus the reality in front of you. Patience has got to be one of the most important life skills that ought to be taught. That chapter was totally left out of the book of my young life.

I was raised by impatient people, and I had internalized that impatience so that there was an innate expectation that things should be done quickly, because God-forbid you had to wait. Within that pressure to be quick was an inherent expectation to be good quickly.

As a child, seeing grownups already successful in their careers or hobbies, I had no idea of the learning curve it took for them to get there. To me at least, it seemed that they were always that way. When I thought the goal was to feel talented and be discovered, rather than just doing something for the sake of doing so because it felt good or got my attention, it did not add up to being a valuable way to spend my time. What I didn't understand was that even if I were talented in some mythical way like I believed people were, I still would have had to develop skills, which was the piece I had left out of the equation I created. It's clear now, but what I didn't know at the time is that a one-and-done mentality is not conducive to learning or creativity.

Being discovered is as much an internal process as an external one.

Discovering our own interests and developing them is one way to truly be seen.

Creativity and art are not the same thing. You can be a creative thinker and an unskilled painter or songwriter.

Your creativity lies where you choose to expand, grow, make new connections, and find unexpected solutions.

Your own life can be the medium of your creative expression.

Chapter 2:

Being Creative is a Skill and a Birthright

My creativity journey led me to a new understanding of, and relationship with, my own creative brilliance. It also taught me about creativity as a whole. I am passionate about walking others through that process so that they can claim and use their own powers. Creativity is not just for special, talented people. It's your birthright.

Creativity expresses itself through the scrappy survivor, the single mom who works and raises kids, the kids who create games and opportunities for themselves, the small town that needs funds for someone's surgery, and in the multitude of ways people solve everyday problems big and small.

Creativity is the essence of the human spirit and a truly necessary skill to survive and thrive. Knowing you can create possibilities for yourself and your family, in any circumstance that is important to you, is a key to feeling safe and empowered. The Creative CORE Method is a tool to help you gain that mastery.

1) *Your ideas about creativity can be expanded*

The Creative CORE Method is for people who want to claim their creativity. What does that mean? Freedom. Possibility. Curiosity. Empowerment. Self-Expression. Time. You Decide...

Whatever it is that you need more of, applying the Creative CORE Method to the problem will open your mind to discovering, crafting, and executing new solutions.

Have you been hindered around the experience of your own creativity? Have you come to believe you're not at all creative or that your creativity doesn't measure up? Do those thoughts bother you? Perhaps you think everyone else is more talented or better than you, and that idea shuts you down. You can use this book to have a new experience.

We human beings are gifted with sentient feelings, critical minds, and imaginations. Each of us is capable of using our creativity to carve out new possibilities. You have the freedom to shift, sort, rearrange, and add elements to your life. You can even re-create your life entirely if you are willing to put in the effort.

This book is the line in the sand, the best tool for when you decide that you want to access your own creativity and feel more alive.

The path you take is up to you. There may be a lot of untangling to do, or it may be some simple tweaks. However, if you have come to the point of feeling trapped, stuck, or curious enough to open a book of this title and resonate with the intention that is written into it, then something inside you is ready for a change. It is time to discover, claim and honor your creative nature.

Creative CORE Method, is a step-by-step system to use. The desired outcome is to introduce you to new creative-thinking abilities. You will also learn which mindsets and ways of thinking can produce more creative results.

Whether you need to solve a simple problem or transform an element of your life, the Creative CORE Method will help you guide yourself through a process to identify ideas you like and develop those ideas into a recipe for action, which you can then execute in order to see your desired changes taking place.

I hope that you will discover not only the pleasure of your own creativity but the power of self-determination, so that you can experience the transformational power of creating with clear alignment and intention.

2) You can imprint the world with your ideas

One of the most potent elements of creativity is that it allows you to intentionally imprint the world with your own ideas and contributions. I think that is why it is such an important experience to grab hold of. Your creative efforts are the gateway between dreams and physical reality.

Every human from the time of birth needs to be seen, recognized, protected, and loved for whom they are. As we grow up, we get thrust into an educational system, the workforce, and many other circumstances that are dictated for us. At some point, the pure ideal of you as the creator of your own life experience can seem a distant dream. As time goes by, you start to wrestle with the certainty of finite quantities of time and space and energy. That awareness can continue to rob your imagination as you just manage the day-to-day elements of life. Or, you can step back, take a breath and consider what you want moving forward.

Maybe you were born to do something that you have not yet scratched the surface of? Maybe you think you need permission to go for it? And maybe this is the moment where you allow yourself to take the first step and ask yourself some questions: What is it? What do I want more of? What do I feel is missing? What do I need to make room for?

If asking such big questions is intimidating and causes your mind to go racing, and all you can see are visions that feel too enormous and heavy to figure out, don't worry. You're not there yet. There is no figuring it out from here. There are steps, questions and processes, uncertainty and, best of all, serendipity. I love the Goethe quote: "Be bold and mighty forces will come to your aid." It always rings true when playing with creativity.

Think about the times you have taken risks, set resolve, and made decisions from the inside-out. Did you experience unexpected results? Remind yourself how things changed or opened up as a result of your efforts. They can be small experiences, as well as large ones.

When you choose to make a change or go out on a limb for something that you want, it requires trust, courage, and inner strength. Sometimes, you get rewarded in the most unexpected ways.

A Serendipity Story

I love it when serendipity shows up and surprises me with the perfect gift. One of my favorite and most magical memories happened in the year 2000. I was a young woman with a small business and some debt. My grandmother had recently passed away and I received a modest inheritance that would pay off that debt almost to the penny. I realized that I was always in debt and didn't like how that felt. I thought it might be smart (and feel good) to wipe out that obligation.

Simultaneously, I was in the throes of deciding whether to take a two-week trip to Bali for a life-changing workshop. It sounded like an amazing opportunity, and my best friend was going, too. I wanted to go so badly but felt conflicted... I was worried about affording the trip and missing work while I was gone. I ultimately decided that I wouldn't go. It seemed irresponsible and counter-productive after just paying off what I owed.

I recall sitting at my desk, feeling my determination to have a fresh start and writing that check to pay off the debt. It was a strange and empowering moment because it was the largest check I had ever written. I stared at it, asking myself "Am I really going to do this, just send this money off?" Yes, I am. I put it in the envelope, walked it to the mailbox, dropped it in and immediately felt a powerful sense of relief. An unexpected feeling of lightness washed over me. My energy felt different; I felt I had made a good choice.

 The next day, out of the blue, I answered a call from an unknown number. They said they were a marketing agency that had been hired to help an international beverage company launch a new bottled water brand. They were tasked with organizing twelve separate events over the span of two weeks throughout Southern California. They needed massage therapists to work at each event and wanted to know if my company would organize and staff the therapists.

I couldn't believe my ears. The launch events were scheduled over the same two weeks as the Bali trip. I did the math and figured out that I could earn enough to cover the cost of the trip while I was away. It was a miracle, something I wouldn't have ever seen coming or even known to ask for. I promptly told the trip's organizer to save me a spot, I was going to Bali. Everything rolled out without a hitch. The Therapists showed up when and where they had agreed to, and I got to see a new country and have a memorable vacation with my best friend.

In retrospect, I couldn't help but feel that the two occurrences– sending off that check and getting the call– were energetically connected. One giant, but uncomfortable, leap of faith opened the door to something unexpected.

Mindset Primer

Serendipity inventory: Make a list of the times good things have happened, doors have opened, invitations have arrived, objects were found or unexpected help arrived.

I keep a serendipity journal just so I can look back to remember fun and unexpected occurrences.

How do you know when it's time to make a change?

Creative "turning point" stories

When I hear the phrase "I don't even know what it means" spoken by my clients, I interpret that as a signal. It means something is brewing. There may be a strong sense of desire, maybe even a start, but not yet a sense of the way through. I don't even know what that means. What a beautiful invitation for creative exploration!

For me, in my story, the "I don't even know what that means" was about creativity itself. I wanted creativity to be at the center of my life, and I didn't know what that meant because I was not an artist.

For my friend Kristen, her *I don't even know* was "I want to work with African Women." She decided to go to Kenya. Once there she asked her cab driver to take her to talk to women. She spent two weeks in the bush, sitting in circles with tribal women and learning about how they didn't have access to clean drinking water. Stunned by this revelation and determined to make a difference, she developed a vision, vowing to come back in a year and drill a water well. Out of that vision came the start of a non-profit, which to date has drilled over 100 wells, bringing water to more than 10,000 people in Samburu in Kenya.

For Mike, a man turning forty and thinking about everything he went through as he matured to this point, his I don't know what it means was "meeting my younger selves." That turned into a question of how could I do that? That question turned into a project where he interacted with and interviewed 40 people, one at each age, in order to help remind him of what it was like. That experience turned into a TedX talk and an entire curriculum for helping empower children and adults improve their self-esteem. He now teaches at schools and corporations while training new people to facilitate the curriculum.

How desire invokes creativity

Let's review the steps these two took through the lens of the CORE Method framework:

Kristen's I don't even know was, "I want to work with African Women."

Reviewing her process, the steps look like this:

COMMUNICATION WITH SELF: How can I know this situation exists and not do anything? I want to come back and bring them water.

OPENING TO IDEAS: Answering the question- How do I help them have water? I will raise money and drill a well.

ROUGH OUT YOUR RECIPE: Come back to the states, educate my network about the problem, present the solution, raise funds, and drill a well.

EXECUTE YOUR PLAN: Raised money, got allies on the ground in Samburu, figured out how to get a well drilled and got it accomplished.

Mike's I don't even know was, "How do I understand myself at earlier ages so I can have compassion and healing now?"

COMMUNICATION WITH SELF: I want to heal my relationship with my past selves.

OPENING TO IDEAS: How can I meet and understand my younger selves?

ROUGH OUT YOUR RECIPE: Tell people about my plan and find access to children and adults at every age who are willing to talk with me about their experiences at that particular stage.

EXECUTE YOUR PLAN: Set up meetings with people at every age I have passed through to witness and observe, have the meetings, and document what I learned.

Reviewing the CORE

A strong desire was communicated within. How the desires would manifest, what shape they would take, or what actions would follow was unknown. They were sitting in an inquiry and open to possibilities in which they answered the questions in the form of ideas. As ideas were presented, the best ones were selected and formed into a rough plan. As they saw the path starting to take shape, each then took steps to execute the plans. As a result of the footwork they did, both found themselves in the midst of new opportunities and situations. They were embodying the creative expression of their desires.

A look at your desires

Do you have an "I don't even know what it means" lurking?

*Note to reader:
This phrase, "I don't even know what it means," may be unclear as you read it.

I keep using it, however, because it is what comes out of people's mouths when they speak to me. If those are not your exact words, listen for your version of that phrase. It might be something like: "I don't know how", or "I'm just not sure."

Another way to approach this idea is to notice if there is a phrase you have repeated to yourself lately, or a desire you had as a younger person that did not make sense. Something you have pushed aside because you did not know what it meant or how you would even do it.

Write it down here:

I want to _____

_____ and I don't even know what that means (meaning you don't know how it would look, come to pass or take shape).

It's just there, now so you have it to remind you and possibly even start to dream about later.

The process of embracing the raw strangeness of your desire and allowing it to permeate you is the kickoff to the creative process.

Urgency vs. Comfort

The raw strangeness of your desire-
Permeating your consciousness
saying
Please, let me do this.
Let's do this, let's have some fun-break out of
the shell
Try something new and different
For God's sake.
Yes.
But I don't know how.
I'm afraid
It's too hard
Too far
Too unknown.
But do you think it's possible?
Yeah, I kinda do.
Then let's!
Just say yes
And we'll see what
unfolds
Do you trust me?
I trust you.
We're one-unified and powered by
The
Great Creator
Let's live into this experience
While alive

Your Urgency vs. Comfort Level

Your lifespan in this body is finite. You know that intellectually, some people live with that awareness front and center, but most don't or it comes and goes based on gains, losses, and close calls. If you have ever met someone that does live with awareness, you notice a clarity and urgency in their words and actions. They are able to drop pretense, cut through to what is most aligned and valuable to them. Decisions and choices are simplified as options are whittled and the mind remains focused.

Have you had any life scares or situations when you saw a window of opportunity closing and were forced to (or chose to) align yourself quickly and accordingly?

It's powerful and empowering to know that kind of radical transformation is available. What got you to the tipping point? Can you recall that urgency now? The newness of it, the starkness? The point of no return?

Manifesting that type of urgency can help your creative process. Through focusing on your vision and clarifying your why, you can cut through excuses to remind yourself what it is you are doing and aid yourself in the process when the going gets tough.

When the desire for a new experience meets the pressure of current circumstances, something has to give. You either give into change, or you give up. When change is the bigger calling, you tip into the realm of the unknown. You'll step through a doorway into the new, and you will navigate as best as you can.

That is where the rubber meets the road in the creative process, where you (E) Execute on a solution. Sometimes you dive in because that is what the situation demands.

However, if you've made your way to this particular book, you are telling yourself that you are ready for a change– yet you want to do it thoughtfully with some sense of control, reason, and intention.

I came to the conclusion that waiting for permission is death. I was killing myself slowly with mind-numbing behaviors around food and drugs in order to cope with the pain that was a result of feeling unrecognized, misunderstood, and overlooked.

The experience I had as a young person was still directing my thinking. Until I woke up in pain and decided that the urgency of now is greater than that story. When I had the presence of mind to look around and inquire whether what I believed was true, I was able to see that it was not. My new question had to become "Where can I contribute?"

I kept waiting to be told where I belonged. Until one day, it hit me like a ton of bricks and I realized I had it all backwards. I needed to dive in and contribute before anyone could really see or guide me. I had to grant myself the permission I was waiting for if I wanted to stop feeling invisible. The words "your visibility is your responsibility" came into my mind and I started saying them to myself as a mantra of encouragement. I grew to understand that by waiting to be seen, I was giving my power away to others by making them responsible for my progress.

It is not fair to expect others to see you if you don't show what you have to offer.

How are the judgments you place against yourself or misunderstandings about the world holding you back?

How I solved the problem of using my creativity

As mentioned in my story earlier in the book, I was walking around feeling deeply overlooked by not ever having my talent identified. I thought everyone else had more knowledge, ability, and value than me. I was essentially living in a constant state of "less than." This led me to playing safe at work and in school. I kept the stakes low and flew under the radar I didn't want anyone to see me try something outside of my comfort zone and make a mistake. Inside I was very sad because there was always a part tucked deep inside that wanted to blossom. The result of this unconscious internal turmoil was a constant state of depression that I didn't even realize existed. To cope, I became a daily cannabis user. I was a raging bulimic for thirteen years. I developed an ability to deflect any questions or inquiries about me, all while keeping a smile on my face and a sense of humor intact.

It's funny the term, "raging bulimic." I realize that it is an angry behavior, but I never read it like that until I just wrote this. Rage, raging. I was furious about this lack of information. I was furious at feeling so insecure all the time, I was furious about not being creative, I was furious about not being talented and that is how I navigated my twenties. I approached my career with the tentativeness of someone who doesn't believe they have anything to offer.

I didn't believe I was smart enough to work for someone

else, so I decided to go out on my own. I studied massage because I had an interest in alternative health and healing. That became my career for 25 years. It served me well because I was great at it, I loved the flexibility of it, and I got to help people feel good at work. I helped clients get back in touch with their bodies, celebrate special occasions, or just plain relax. I worked at a top spa and felt proud of that. I had my own company that took me to movie sets to work on directors and actors. I had a crew that went to offices; we helped bring forth the concept of on-site massage. I was even interviewed by international media when I had a crew at the 2000 Democratic National Convention in Los Angeles.

There were a lot of good elements of that career, yet inside I felt dissatisfied. If I am honest, I think my ego never felt quite gratified enough. Many times, at parties someone would ask what I do, I would tell them and they'd say, "oh," and walk away. Worse, they'd turn around and expect me to rub their shoulders, saying something like, "Here, give a sample." No thank you. I always thought to myself, the man of my dreams would say, "oh, you must need a shoulder rub" and offer me one. I haven't met the man of my dreams yet, well at this age I should say the man of my reality. so that still may or may not happen.

The point is that my career solved a lot of my personal challenges even though it did not give me the creativity or intellectual stimulation I craved. I would be saying to myself that I wanted more creativity in my life, wanted something different, to be more stimulated intellectually, and I was very much at a loss as to what I could do next. I felt stuck in a pigeonhole with such a specific skill set. This was me in the first phase of the C portion of the

CORE process, communicating with myself. It was something that happened over a period of time.

Over time this conflict wore me down. My turning point came one night in something that felt like a breakdown. I was tired and I simply bottomed out. I found myself crying on the living room floor. It was a deep cry of grief, loss, desperation, and surrender. Everything I had been holding in came rushing out in guttural cries and exhausted tears. In the midst of it, I heard myself saying out loud, "I want to be uniquely me, I want to be recognized for it, I want to hold space for transformation, I want to support others' creativity, I want creativity at the center of my life and I have no idea what that means." This was a moment of a clarified vision, the outcome of the **C, COMMUNICATION WITH SELF.**

As I laid there sobbing, knowing that I was not going to spend the next X number of years dedicating myself to learning painting, taking up the guitar, or becoming an actress (all the things I thought creativity meant), a question bubbled up: "I wonder if there is such a thing as a graduate program in creativity?" Turning that clarified vision into a question caused me to pop into the next step of **O, OPENING TO IDEAS.**

When I stopped crying, I Googled "graduate programs creativity" and I found two. I researched them both and applied to the oldest one, at Buffalo State College in New York. I got accepted and honestly, I did not understand the program; it kept talking about Creative Problem Solving. I had no idea what it was, but it was creative and that is what I wanted, so off I went for a new adventure. This was me being in process with the **R, ROUGHING OUT THE RECIPE** step, building on the idea I selected as a solution. The rest was **E, EXECUTE YOUR PLAN** and how I maneuvered through that over time.

The program was very disorienting at first because I had to wrap my mind around a new framework for what creativity was, what it looked like, and how it worked. I needed to embrace a new world view, and that takes some getting used to.

Once I understood what they were talking about, I could see that what I was learning was exactly the answer I was seeking: how to have creativity at the center of my life. I went from having no idea what that meant, to seeing a new path forward. One that would allow me to teach others who, like me, felt stuck and beholden to their circumstances because of the expectations surrounding them– feeling safe, but not necessarily right.

I started leading workshops for people like me who harbored ideas that their creativity was inaccessible, or even non-existent. I called the class Creativity for Personal Transformation; it attracted people who were navigating a transition and wanted to experience more authentic expression in their lives.

This book is here to help you re-evaluate your relationship to your creativity and to consider new possibilities around what is next for you.

Once you open up your perceptions and recognize that creativity includes the way you approach problem-solving, navigate change, and interact with your life, you have given yourself permission to own the process and make it uniquely your own.

Chapter 3:

How Do You Become a Creative?

Did you pick up this book because you wanted to have time for more creative projects? Are you finally making time to do the artistic pursuits you have always imagined you would like to do when you had more time?

Perhaps you are attracted to the idea of transforming an area of your life, using a creative process, and coming out with your life improved: be it work, health, or relationships.

My intention for the book is to offer creative thinking as a guide for intentional change. However, you can use the process to empower yourself and make room in your life for the artistic endeavors you want to return to, asking yourself questions like how might I make room in my life for x,y,or z?

You will need to develop your skills beyond reading this book, along with persistence and willingness to keep developing through the learning curve. This is going to take commitment.

I'd like you to consider three big skills that enhance creativity as you read this book:

- *Your open-minded curiosity*

- *Your ability to tolerate uncertainty*

- *Your willingness to be in process*

Creativity and art are not the same thing.

For the purposes of this book, let's un-couple the idea that artistic means being creative or vice-versa. The essence of the lesson in this book is that your thinking can be creative. The many ways you express and apply that thinking becomes the evidence of your creativity. If you are a person who says, "I don't have a creative bone in my body," I beg to differ. You may not express yourself the same way as someone you think of as wildly creative or artistic, but that does not mean you don't have your own capacity to meet challenges with creative solutions. Following the steps in this book can give you an experience of what that means. You may, or may not, have artistic aspirations. If you do, you may want to use the process in this book to figure out how to experience more of your artistic expression in your life- and that is a fine vision.

The intended outcome of this book is for you to experience the power of developing a creative mindset that can be applied to any area of your life.

Changes you see as a result of the work you do in this book are the expression of your creativity in process.

You can create more of whatever it is you want to experience in life. If what you want to do is make a life change, career change, dive into an idea you have been harboring, maybe you need to improve your social life, start a hobby, even declutter a closet, anywhere there is room for change you can use the process.

As you begin to embody the understanding of why and how creativity and art are not the same thing, the next time someone asks you if you are creative, you can answer with a confident YES!

You'll have firsthand understanding of the affirmation:

I am creative and the satisfaction I experience in my life is a reflection of how I use that creativity.

Why being creative can seem so scary to your parents

Creativity can be like a mythical sea monster, out there ready to attack and drown you. There are legends about famous artists who have suffered and died for their art, like Van Gogh cutting off his ear… There are so many ideas about what creativity should be and what it says about a person.

You've been told myths like, "you have to be crazy to be creative, you have to starve, you have to go off alone, you have to suffer for your art, you need drugs to access it, the muse has to come, nobody ever makes a living doing what they love," or those that do are "few and far between."

For many parents, those myths are their worst nightmare for their child who plans on being a rockstar or painter. "Those are nice hobbies but making a living doing that is for other people, not my child. Get a job."

The thing is that in some circumstances, all of those fears are true. People do suffer for their art. There are lots of starving artists. Certain elements of the creative mindset also show up in mental illness. Some people take drugs and create art. Others will toil in oblivion for their art. There are no guarantees.

This book is not meant to convince you to leave your family and go spend the next ten years under a palm tree learning to paint (unless you do the work around your vision and realize that what is next for you is palm-tree painting).

Clearly what you come up with is beyond the scope of a book.

Your truth is your truth. I am simply offering an approach to adopting a creative mindset and creative process that will allow you to think more flexibly about your life. Consider how you may use creativity to change it and have more of what you want.

How to get to know your creativity in a non-threatening way.

This book is geared towards a practical form of creativity, my hope for you is that creativity feels more inviting and accessible as you start to engage with the process. If you have solved a problem in daily life, looked for a novel solution at work, or helped a child create a school project, then you know you have experienced using your creativity in a practical and positive way.

I was facilitating the CORE process from the stage during a short talk at a conference. At the end, people shared. One lady was completely lit up about what she created for herself, about cleaning her closets so she and her daughter could live together more easily. I include this because it's important to realize that you can apply this thinking to smaller tasks. Anywhere you feel stuck may benefit from new thinking. There's something liberating that happens when you shift the way you look at problems. They seem to loosen up and become solvable.

You can be creative and sane!

You may feel like you are losing your marbles as you venture into uncharted territory. It's unsettling and there may be times where you question your choices, but if it's done as part of the process - with grounding, with reason, and with purpose – then you're probably not crazy; you're just trying to navigate the unknown. Sometimes we equate uncertain choices with insanity. Change can be scary; and making an unexpected change doesn't mean you're crazy.

Are you so busy that you don't have time to consider how you might be creative?

If you think you might be too busy and your life is too overwhelming to consider how you might have more creativity, then it's time to apply some creative thinking to the problem of not enough time so that you can have a new experience.

By embracing your creativity, you can empower others to be creative too.

When you start to appreciate the power of your creativity and see what possibilities it opens for you, then you begin to understand how you can empower others the same way. By holding space for possibility in your own mind and life, a habit develops, and you can offer others the same support for their own creative evolution.

You don't have to starve to be a creative person.

By relinquishing the idea that starving and creativity go together, you can allow yourself the opportunity to explore how it can be integrated in a manageable way that rounds out your life, instead of the creative process taking over and consuming you.

Your creativity can be based on your values and meaning. You choose it. It does not choose you. This approach to creativity is meant to round out and evolve your life. With this approach to transformation, you can move forward knowing your actions are based on your values, planning, and wisdom.

You can give yourself permission to expand your sense of possibility and increase your self-expression in life. You can share your voice, your point of view, your passion, and be seen for how creative you are already.

Chapter 4:

A Look at The Creative Process

If you have traversed a change with an uncertain outcome, you have traveled the steps of the creative process.

You may not realize it now, but if you were to look back and plot your choice points and then identify the steps, you would see that there was a path. That path, for the most part, matched the process I'm about to share with you.

When I looked back at a time of transition in my life, when I changed careers, I realized that I had applied the creative process. I didn't know it at the time, but after I studied creativity, I could see it was so. Being able to identify that process became empowering because it provided a container with reference points for how to move forward, and what the appropriate next steps would be. I also learned in the process that there were times when I just wasn't going to know what was next, and I had to persevere anyway. Those moments became exciting because they were invitations for serendipity to surprise and support me.

An example of an unexpected nudge in the right direction happened for me when I volunteered to lead an improvisational movement class during free time at a retreat I was attending. One of the participants ended up thinking it would be a great class to teach at the Santa Barbara City College extension. She gave me some contact information and I followed up on it right away. I was told NO to that class, but they came back with an alternative offer. If I could teach a comedy improv class, I could have a spot. I had studied just enough comedy improvisation to say "yes, I can do that." That was how I ended up teaching improvisation to seniors and how I first began to synthesize my approach to teaching creativity with the use of improvisation. When I look back, I can see that this all aligned with my stated vision of doing something unique that had creativity at the center of it.

When I was first introduced to the concept that creativity is a thinking skill and that the process of creating follows a natural course, I was thrown off and skeptical. That new orientation was so different from my lifelong perception, that I initially fought it because I did not understand. It didn't make sense to my worldview. I was too focused on the type of outcome as the evidence of creativity. I thought it meant I had to be an artist. I knew I couldn't be the only one who didn't get this distinction.

However, once I started to get into the groove of understanding the larger perspective, I got excited and the lightbulb went on! When that happened, my question became, "How can I share this understanding with others?" This perspective is empowering because it opens the doorway to answering the question: how am I creative even if I am not an artist?

Once you know the steps of the creative process, you will have perspective that can help you determine what to do next.

By learning and working with the Creative CORE Method, you can develop the ability to shift perspective, going between a micro and macro perspective.

Giving yourself a bird's eye view can be a comforting skill since so much of the creative process can feel unknown. A major element of being in the middle of the creative process is adapting to a level of uncertainty.

Ambiguity is how that uncertainty is referred to in the scholarly circles of those who study creativity. The attribute is called Tolerance of Ambiguity. (TOA)

Ambiguity exists because there is always a time in your process when you are metaphorically between the two shores, and you just have to keep swimming forward. That time in the middle can be filled with doubt and can be stressful- causing you to question your choices and actions. You think you're moving one direction, but the current could be pulling you off course.

Maybe your course needs adjustment, maybe your goal needs a bit of tweaking. The creative process is full of adjustments; how you stay the course vs. how it will change is unknown. Eventually you will be able to look back, review what happened, and see how you arrived at what you are doing now.

That in between time is when it is so important to not give up, not allow the voices of fear, judgment, and doubt to overtake you. Don't let it convince you to quit.

Rather, it is the time to dig into recalling your vision,

your why, opening your senses to invite in the elements of grace and serendipity.

Persist. Find your grit, lean in, and know you are in process.

Sometimes the process can look different on different days. Sometimes it looks like taking your foot off the gas by taking a walk, taking a break, or giving yourself time away. You may find that during one of those breaks you feel guilty because you're browsing the internet, listening to the radio, calling a friend... when an unexpected piece of information is revealed! Just as you are telling yourself, "I'm wasting time and doing nothing.," boom! What you need to see, know, or learn comes into your awareness.

Develop a mindset of allowing for those moments and trusting they will occur. They are exhilarating, making you feel supported like The Universe has got your back and wants you to keep moving on. It is the reason I like to keep a serendipity journal because it reminds me that good things happen in unexpected ways.

*Keep a serendipity journal.

When surprising things happen that you didn't expect but were just what you needed, write them down and say thanks.

Suggested Affirmation

I am supported and connected to all of life.

I keep my eyes and ears open knowing that whatever I need I can find, or it can find me.

I I am taken care of, and I am grateful for that.

Building Your Creative CORE Strength

Let's start by seeing The Creative CORE Method in action. I will be using my process and my story as an example.

I, Vivian, have a simmering problem with my life. I know I don't want to do the work I am doing anymore. I don't feel intellectually challenged, my body hurts, I feel I have more to give. I have this idea that I want more creativity in my life, I want to do something unique and different. I am circling and I don't know what to do.

Here is the invitation to start with the first step: C - COMMUNICATION WITH SELF.

I sit with myself in inquiring what is it that i want. I get responses, I keep writing and suddenly this very clear vision comes together: I want to do something unique; I want creativity at the center of my life, and I don't even know what that means.

That was **C, COMMUNICATION WITH SELF**, and it generated the vision of having creativity at the center.

Problem: I have no idea what that means (given the

information I have at this moment in time and my understanding of creativity).

Great! Now you have a clarified question to bring into **O - OPENING TO IDEAS**.

How can I have creativity be the center of my life? I naturally start to open to ideas: What could that mean? How might I do it? Is it even possible?

I begin to generate ideas, to answer these questions and bridge the gap between a not creative life and having creativity at the center of my life. Thoughts that emerged looked like: learn an art form, learn music, become an art teacher, volunteer for an organization that delivers art as healing to others, take on a hobby, learn more about what creativity means.

Learning more about what creativity actually means grabs my attention. I decide to do more research.

Boom! This pops you into the next step: **R - ROUGHING OUT YOUR RECIPE**.

Research brings up more questions: maybe I'll study creativity professionally. Is there a graduate program in creativity? If education is what I select, what schools are available to me? I look for a program that interests me.

Now it's time for the fourth and final step in The Creative Core Method: **E - EXECUTE YOUR PLAN**.

My research has led me to a program that I find compelling, I think I should apply.

I apply to grad school with the intention that, after I

receive this education, I will have a foundation to confidently figure out a way to have creativity be the center of my life.

There you have it:

- COMMUNICATION WITH SELF
- OPENING TO IDEAS
- ROUGHING OUT YOUR RECIPE
- EXECUTING YOUR PLAN

The result I created from following what I now call The Creative CORE Method was the formation of a new understanding and relationship to creativity. My transformed relationship with creativity enabled me to go back into the process and rough out a new recipe to a new question:

How can I do something unique to me, and make creativity the center of my life? The recipe I landed on was to develop a coaching practice, teach, and write a book about the creative process. (That's this book by the way).

You can see from this example that the creative process is a cycle of evolution. Once you know the CORE steps, you will be able to navigate to the right place within the process to get yourself moving again and to continue growing.

I hope that my example whets your appetite, and that you start to ask yourself questions about what you need or want (Spoiler alert: coming up next).

Try looking back on your own life to recognize how you have already used creative thinking to traverse change. Think back to a problem you solved and see if you can identify your CORE steps. Recognizing you have already used The Creative CORE Method empowers you to feel excited about your own creativity in a new and fresh way.

The CORE process gives you the opportunity to go deep, when there is time to sit with a question and make sure your actions are aligned with your highest values.

Sometimes our need to change is immediate. In those urgent or unexpected times, the mindset skills we use in the creative process will help you think on your feet.

All your experiences can be used for learning when you have the attitude of identifying and applying the takeaways. From the creativity perspective, those insights drive iteration, which is essentially going back to the drawing board, figuring out what worked, what didn't, tweaking an aspect, and trying again.

When you follow the steps of the full CORE process, take the time to create your vision, then do the exercises that ground them in your values; you will be starting from a solid foundation and setting a trajectory that will increase the likelihood of a satisfactory outcome. Time spent up front pays off on the back end because you have taken the time to listen to your heart, and you have paid attention to your own inspiration. If along the way you need to make adjustments, it is all part of the process. There is a concept called iteration and it is as much of the creative process as generating ideas.

Iteration is a new and improved version - starting the process over with new adjustments in place, midway through the process. It's what business today refers to as failing fast and often, getting a product out there, seeing what works, and then fixing the identified problems before putting another version out there. I see this a lot with the entrepreneurs I work with while developing their products and marketing: try something; if it doesn't work, tweak it, and try again.

By sharing your creative ideas, you can find partners who can help you achieve your dream.

When you decide it's time to make a change now and start to take steps to do so, remember that creativity benefits from collaboration. Two minds or more can be better than one in identifying interesting solutions by pulling ideas and concepts from different areas of expertise. Be willing to find partners to support your change, and if you need to find new people to support you– go find them. Sometimes those closest to us are threatened by our plans or worry about how they will fit into your new plans. Be mindful of who you enroll in supporting your plans.

Think about people who have your best interest at heart, who want to see you succeed, and are willing to see you in your potential, not just as they have known you. Be honest with yourself about who your allies are and are not. Your change can be uncomfortable for others. It may mean readjusting, and humans like to be comfortable. We like reliability and we like our loved ones to remain predictable so we can feel safe.

If you're ready for change and others around you are not ready to see you change, marshal some outside forces to support you, that's all I'm saying.

Chapter 5:

Perspective Shift:

Prepare Yourself to Create

Creativity starts at the intersection of problems and thinking skills.

By now you are likely understanding creativity a bit differently than when you started this book. You can see it as a skill and birthright that is innately human. As you work through this book, you will gain a deeper appreciation of your creativity by continuing to acknowledge it and learning how to apply it with intentionality. You will use it to guide yourself into solutions that help you meet whatever challenge you are currently facing.

This shift also helps when someone comes to you asking for help with their problem. Instead of trying to solve it for them, you can ask questions that encourage their creative thinking and help them have a breakthrough for themselves.

We will get into the four steps: **COMMUNICATION WITH SELF, OPENING TO IDEAS, ROUGHING OUT YOUR RECIPE and EXECUTING YOUR PLAN** and talk about mindsets that will support your momentum during the process. Knowledge of mindsets is important because there is a degree of uncertainty while you are in the creative change process. If you're not prepared for handling that experience, it may derail you by leading you to believe that you're better off quitting, you're not doing it right, or you picked the wrong thing. Being able to stay objective in order to overcome that kind of destructive self-talk is imperative to bridging the gap of where you are to where you want to be.

The nature of your journey through The Creative CORE may seem unclear at first. It's like learning how to dive and swim simultaneously. Over time and with practice it will make sense.

In part 2, you will do an exercise of deconstructing a process you already lived through. That reflection will provide an opportunity to recognize where your thinking skills and questions occurred while you were in the process. This will enable you to see for yourself that your creativity is in place. The difference as you move forward will be that you are navigating change with a compass. You will also have empowering questions to ask yourself along the way. You'll be mindful of the importance of taking time to develop your solution, and you will understand that managing uncertainty is key to a successful outcome.

How not to undermine yourself

When working with clients and talking to people who aren't completely clear on what they are moving toward, I see that they are prone to believing that nothing is happening, that they're wasting time, or not doing it right. These thoughts can occur because circumstances are not showing up in the outside world in the timeframe or way that the person wants.

When a piece of information or desired assistance is not forthcoming, or an opportunity is not right there when you need it, it can feel frustrating. Some people will blame themselves, while others just throw up their hands and say, "It's not in the cards." Then there are those who will just keep changing course, looking for "the thing" when they haven't stuck to the original solution long enough to allow it to work.

Having good friends, trustworthy colleagues, or a coach who can see your blind spots is important. If you tend to fall into the behavior of giving up, or tend towards defeatist thinking, get your support lined up ahead of time. This is why the EXECUTE YOUR PLAN step asks you to identify the people who will be on your side assisting you along the way.

Iteration is part of creation (a.k.a. If at first you don't succeed try, try again)

All that being said, solutions are never a one and done situation. Life is too unpredictable. Sometimes you do need to change course and rearrange. The point is to make those changes from a place of clarity and responsiveness, not just as reactions to elements not coming together the way you planned at the time you planned.

Discernment and honest evaluation are your friends. You may need to change course, or maybe you just need to take a timeout, allow yourself a walk in the woods or at the beach. Give yourself a real timeout to listen to the radio, take a random dive on the internet, or catch up with a friend. Sometimes you will be led to the information or answer at a time or place you did not expect it.

I am a strong believer in serendipity. I encourage you to invite serendipity into your process. If you imagine serendipity as a fun, helpful energy that is there to add surprise, delight, and assistance to your process, it just makes it a little more exciting. Imagine that there is some energy out there that will meet you and add a little spark of support when you least expect it.

Focus + Action + Serendipity = Surprising opportunities and solutions.

Those sparks of support are the delight of creativity; you don't know exactly where you'll end up.

You just keep answering questions, putting pieces in place, and realigning your direction to make sure you're pointed in the direction you want to go. Think of the process as a conversation with possibility, that you are in a constant feedback loop until you get where you're going. Then you get to begin again. That is the wonder of being alive. It never stops being possible to play with life. That is why I always say Creativity is Life and Life is Creative. If you are above ground, there is something possible for you.

There is a gentle way to open yourself to a meditative, mindful state. The Creative CORE process provides access to an experience of being connected to the infinite space that exists all around you. When you can really include infinite possibility as your co-creator in a project or process, it becomes fun to submerge yourself in the mindset that anything is possible in any areas where you may be stuck or don't know what you want to create.

You can start to think about how to have more creativity in your life, or how to adapt your life so that it feels more creative

As you move forward, I hope you are excited by the opportunities you see to become a more creative person. You may choose to rearrange, substitute, and replace elements of your life and that might be difficult or intimidating, but you will do it from a grounded place that is congruent and aligned with your values and vision.

Can you release your need to be rich and famous, and enjoy your creativity?

If the idea of fame has shaped your perceptions of the value of your own creative endeavors, think about the messages you received from your parents, or even your peers. I have come to believe that putting a prerequisite expectation of garnering a high level of public validation for your creative work to feel valuable is an abdication of your birthright. This type of pressure can short-circuit and erase the intrinsic pleasure and developmental benefits that come from exploring or playing with your creative expression just for the sake of it.

Release the need for greatness and replace it with appreciation for the experience of being engaged and for growth, learning, brain stimulation and fun.

I had a client who said she wanted to sing. She also wanted to be famous. She didn't believe she could become famous and so used that idea as an excuse to not sing.

After we talked, she realized that she was not allowing herself the experience of her own self-expression. She recognized that wanting to be famous caused her to limit her opportunities to participate where she could and miss out on any chance of being recognized at whatever level she was at.

Digging deeper there was probably a layer of fear of not being good enough and that is an Achilles heel of creativity.

Since this book is focused on creativity and personal transformation, I ask you to take the steps to do activities and make changes for yourself first. Once you admit you want to do something, and you overcome the excuses as to why you shouldn't or you can't, you can start to carve out ways to make it possible.

How can you open to the possibility that there is a way for you to engage and have more?

The time is now. Do you feel that there are activities, actions, endeavors, or purposes that have been lying dormant inside you? Do you have sensations that you cannot shake and the feeling that you should pay attention? If you just haven't known where to start, then you got the right book. If you follow the path and keep an open mind, you can have a different experience.

What about greatness, talent, fame, and money?

Yes, what about them? Are fame and money what you want? Is that the end to which you are aiming your creative energies? If so, what vehicle are you using to get there? Does that desired outcome affect your willingness to engage with the activity? Can you enjoy the activity for the sake of the activity?

If the desire for fame and the need for recognition prevents you from enjoying something you might be good at and like doing, you might want to rethink your priorities and ask yourself if the activity is worth doing only in front of others or doing alone. Let's face it, even if you are going to achieve fame, you'd have to start in obscurity anyway. You can't be famous until you do the thing, so you may as well do it because you want to.

Putting your feelings of success in the hands of another to recognize and value you is giving your power away to others. Much of the media today would have us believe that our value is in our purse and how we get paid. Yes, that is how we survive, but we also need to claim our voices and our right to build our lives around that which feels meaningful and good to the spirit.

Even if you love it, building skill does not always feel good.

In deciding to write this book I had to come to a place where every day I had to declare: no more excuses, you're going to write this book- even if it's not a bestseller. I had to choose to write myself through the portal of becoming an author. I faced the demons of resistance, the doubt, the judgment and the "who am I to..." It's all part of the process. Just get yourself into the process so you can begin.

It's your turn. Claim your right to your creativity, your self-expression, and your ability to transform your desires into reality. Start by sharing it out loud.

**You can join the Facebook Group at
https://www.facebook.com/groups/creativecorebook
and let us know what you're up to.**

**Or tag us on Instagram @creativitymuse
https://www.instagram.com/creativitymuse/**

Let us see and hear you now.

Chapter 6:

Your Dream vs. The Prescribed Path

America has been such a unique experiment, a place where freedom and the pursuit of happiness and religious freedom are bedrock values. Being born here, I didn't know anything else. Being raised in Southern California in the 70s, I was steeped in the tea of acceptance of sharing feelings, self-discovery, activities that used to be termed crunchy or granola. I didn't know anything different.

We were just aiming to be happy and to be the best versions of ourselves.

My father was a first generation American, born here. He was a veteran and went to law school on the GI Bill. He was very grateful for the opportunity to receive an education, and worked hard to provide for his family so we had a comfortable life and a traditional structure. My mother did not work outside of the house while I was growing up. When it was time for me to get out and get a job, he was always suggesting things that were not creative, that sounded like death to me.

I used to get so resentful and hurt because he seemed to not "get" or see me, and it felt like an insult and a slight that he would suggest such things to me.

They would be in the vein of administrative-type things

and from the outside, all those words said to me was your creative spirit is dead.

For many years I felt injured by my father and his practical advice. It was a wound that lingered until one day I was talking to a wise friend. After telling her about it she said: "You know, it was not his job to worry about your creativity. It was his job to make sure you could feed yourself after he was dead."

With that reframe, everything shifted. I knew she was right. Of course, my father was looking at the world as he understood it with the reliable rules that he learned. Following those rules got him to safety and enabled him to provide a stable life for us. That was what he wanted for me. He loved me and wanted to know that I could be self-sufficient without him and to him that looked like following a known career path.

There was another truth I suffered with, which I did not express because I didn't know it could be any different. That truth was that I felt like a misfit. I struggled to get certain types of work done and it made me feel stupid. I am just realizing that the constant accommodations I had to make for myself to get anything done were where the bulk of my creative energies went; maybe that is why my family didn't see me as creative. Nobody knew what I was dealing with. I didn't ask for help because I didn't know I was struggling–to me, it had always been that way. It wasn't until well into my forties that I was diagnosed with ADHD. In retrospect, that was why I felt I had to fashion my own path. I had to find a way where all my shortcomings could be accommodated. As I mentioned earlier in my story, I found my solution by becoming a Massage Therapist and starting a business that I ran for twenty-three years.

Problem Solving in Action

If you wrap this piece back around to the lens of creativity and problem solving and then zoom out a bit, you can frame the problem I needed to solve as: how do I have work I like, where I feel confident and am not micromanaged?

Massage Therapy became my unexpected but workable solution. I was not micromanaged, got to work in my own style, was accountable to my client for 50 minutes to 80 minutes, and that was that. The work also satisfied my lifelong interest in health and the healing arts. I didn't have to show up for a standard 40-hour week, which gave me flexibility, and I got to help people feel good while contributing to their wellbeing. The work, although not necessarily creative, was unique because each person received their own experience and I got to pour my heart into it. Massage was a great solution for my situation until I burned out. Once I had reached that point, I realized I desired the opportunity to apply my intellect differently. I also needed to give my body a break.

*A special note to practical people: But what if it's not practical?

One of the main challenges and original inspirations for this book was the case of the practical person. The ones who were raised to check off the boxes and create a secure life for themselves following a prescribed path that may not have aligned with their actual interests.

In their effort to abide by their parents' or society's expectations, they may have cut off some part of themselves so they could channel themselves into the path prescribed. It is those people whose ears I want to whisper into and encourage. Play, explore, see what wants to come out and explore. If the identity you have created or the life you have in place is too rigid to allow such endeavors, yet you're reading this book, open the door to yourself, answer the questions in this text and allow your imagination to roam.

People who seek me out tend to be successful, accomplished, and have oftentimes put so much of their life force energy into careers and commitments around those careers, there is simply little time left to nurture the creative process. It's really scary to consider how to extricate one's energy if you think it has to be an all or nothing approach. That is where the coaching, the teasing out what's possible, the pulling it apart little by little, looking for cracks, identifying assumptions, and preparing internally for the experience that might happen if letting people down all need to be walked through.

Dismantling does not have to look like blowing the whole house down in one fell swoop. I like to say, pull it apart before it falls apart...if that is what you're called to do. That is why there are steps, and the first step of listening (to yourself) is there. You enter this process with clarity, it's grounded.

It's the difference between the idea of the crazy creative vs the thoughtful intentional person. The thoughtful intentional person has decided that they are ready to make room for some new energy and experience in their lives. They then examine fearlessly how to do it so they can create the time and put their attention onto something else that they value but have not made a priority. No experience is ever wasted. The energy, effort, connections, worldliness, power, prestige, financial security: all that you have created is there to serve you.

You own it all. The wisdom is within you and you bring it with you, adding depth and intelligence to whatever your next steps become. You've done so well already. The attributes that got you where you are today can be repurposed into the next phase.

What the idea of safety is all about and how it confines us

We do need to walk a fine line between being productive and able to meet our own needs for safety and security, but does it have to operate like your parents' model of the world? I don't know.

Perhaps if you have the freedom to ask this question, you have come to a place where you can choose for yourself and now embark on a path that might be a more satisfying trajectory. Or maybe you just incorporate pieces of you that need more attention and expression.

When I encourage you to connect to your creativity, I am asking you to connect to the essence of your spirit, your heart, and your light. Think of your creativity as a line to the highest possible you and invite that experience in when you are in the process of answering questions and thinking about what's next. Consider that your heart is a real force for good, and deciding how to share it is your offering to the world.

How our society is changing requires more creativity. Systems are changing and some are not coming back. How will you navigate, re-invent, and find alternative solutions?

When you look around the world today, it may seem that the narratives and structures that our parents and grandparents relied on, and that you were raised believing in, are no longer the reliable solutions they once were. You may feel a general malaise or just feel unsettled and not know what to do next. That is the wheelhouse of the Creative CORE journey.

You might not know exactly where you're headed and that might scare the heck out of you. It is understandable, and you can choose to empower yourself with these tools. Manage your mindset, speak up, find allies, and become open to the many resources that you probably have at your fingertips.

Part 2:

Generate Solutions
and Decide

Chapter 7:

Access and Use Your Creative CORE

Your body has a core of muscles that keep you balanced, flexible, erect, and mobile. These qualities enable you to meet the demands of physical movement in your day-to-day life. You adjust your balance, lift weight, pivot, flex, bend and move yourself forward as needed. As you visualize all these maneuvers, imagine that your thinking has those same capacities.

You can shift perspective, pivot thought streams, adjust approaches, flex your thinking to go deeper into new territories, make new connections, find analogies, generate questions. These are core movements of creative thinking. By becoming aware of and strengthening these skills as mental muscles you flex at will, your mental agility and ability to meet challenges creatively can improve.

When situations arise that require you to shift directions– like when a colleague or spouse suggests adding a new dimension to something you have been working on and you just don't see it at first– instead of having a knee-jerk reaction that says no, you can receive the input and then ask yourself (and them) questions, which might help you see the challenge through a variety of lenses. You may be asked to discard ideas you love to come up with new ones, and maybe a little tweak will be all it takes to elevate. One never knows, but this way of being flexible allows you to be inclusive, open, and collaborative.

Just like you work the muscles of your body to keep your core strength, you can do so for your mind and, in turn, keep your creative strength alive. Applying the tools of The Creative CORE Method helps you focus on the creative process and keep your mind flexible and limber. This way you can be creatively fit, as well as physically.

This approach to creativity removes some of the mystery and separation that generally makes the "normal" person feel different from the artist. There is some glamor, allure and mystery to their process, but there is also hard work, dedication, trying and failing, then trying again–all while incorporating new ideas and working in service of a vision. They follow the same underlying process in the creation of their work. When you strip away the vehicle for the expression, the steps are the same.

The CORE Method of creativity is directly inspired by the Creative Problem-Solving Model.

CPS for short. The CPS model has been in use for over half a century. It was originated by a man named Alex Osborne, who was the "O" in the famous television advertising agency BBDO. CPS has been used in business to create products and processes.

As I was learning it, it became apparent to me that by understanding creativity as a process through the lens of a model, it stopped being a mysterious talent that only some people have. In other words, the CPS model is an applicable workhorse that you can apply to personal challenges, to the creation of art, or products for commerce.

As a coach who supports people in connecting with and expressing their authentic truths, it became the perfect vehicle to focus my teaching and practice.

The CPS model taught me that the creative process follows a natural rhythm. Like day follows night, if you're in the dark, you know eventually dawn will arrive. Once you learn the steps of the Method, you can locate yourself in it.

If you are stuck in one part of the process, say circling on an idea, you can say to yourself: "I need to go back and revisit the communication and clarification stage and figure out if my vision is clear enough." You may need to move forward to ROUGHING OUT YOUR RECIPE. With a roughed-out recipe, you have some clear actions you can then go on to execute.

One challenge many people face when manifesting their creative efforts is trying to do too many things on their own.

When you get clear on your vision, it excites and motivates you. It becomes much easier to share that vision and enroll people to support and help you along the way. In the same way that your vision pulls you forward, it has the potential to draw others in.

Reflecting on Creativity

When you look back on the choices you have made in your life and see how situations unfolded, you may be able to identify how the creative thinking process was present during previous times of change.

The following process is reflective. Use it as a tool to identify a specific time in the past where you unknowingly followed the Creative CORE steps. Doing the exercise will empower you because you will recognize that all the tools you'll look at- brainstorming, synthesizing, clarifying, making a plan, and taking action-are all skills you are familiar with. You will see for yourself that when they are employed in a directed order with intention, creative change happens.

Thought Exercise: Reverse engineer a situation

Get a pen so you can write the answers in the book in the spaces below, or you can simply reflect.

Remember a time when you made an important or unexpected change, one that at its outset you were not sure how you would navigate it.

Look for the first step, the **C: COMMUNICATION WITH SELF**.

- What were you saying to yourself?
- What were you seeing or feeling?
- What did you need?
- How did you know it was time to change?
- Can you identify a statement of desire that became crystal clear?
- Was there a phrase you had to act upon?

Write the phrase down as it came to at that time.

- With that communication in mind, did ideas start to emerge as a result?

- Were you generating many thoughts about how you could answer the call of your crystalized desire?

- Were you having conversations with others, soliciting ideas and asking for their perspectives?

That was you moving into the **O, OPENING TO IDEAS** step. you can write some of the ideas or the main idea that you moved forward with below.

- Think about how the various ideas came together and became the ingredients for the recipe you worked to bring to life. These were the elements you thought you could move forward with.

- Can you recall coming up with steps and plans?

That was you moving into the **R, ROUGHING OUT YOUR RECIPE**.

Write down some of the steps of the plan you came up with for how you were going to get from idea to execution, so that you can see your roughed out recipe:

_____

_____

_____

Reviewing the recipe that you came up with in the previous step, think about your first steps. Remember how you began to take action, or E, EXECUTE YOUR PLAN, along with the help you got, the tools you put in place, the way you spoke about your intentions.

- What did you do?

_____

_____

_____

As you can see from this exploration, you can identify the flow and the process. This is how you implemented The Creative CORE Method in a situation.

I hope this helped you feel even more confident in your ability to think creatively so that you approach the rest of this process with curiosity and enthusiasm.

Are you approaching Life or is Life approaching you?

There is a song by the band Talking Heads called "Once in a Lifetime." The song's chorus would often repeat in my head as I was writing this book. The song asks the question "How did I get here?" The answer is "letting the days go by" as the singer refers to his beautiful house, his beautiful wife. Have you ever felt that way? Wondering how did you get here? I did, and I must admit that fear was a big culprit. However, developing confidence in my creativity gave me courage to take more risks as I progressed in life.

Expectations

Are you where you are in life by intention as a creative act, or have you let the days go by? Have you stumbled along the way led by a sense of duty to others, fulfilling someone else's plan? Or were you trying to escape the situation you came from, never to repeat it? Whatever your answer is, I truly, deeply respect you and your process. Whatever you have achieved or haven't achieved that you might think you could or should have, please leave it at the door. Be kind and gentle. I truly believe we are all doing the best we can in the moment even if we don't like it. Even if we could/should/ought to be doing better or different. If it's truly your heart's desire, and you are willing to act, your future will demonstrate it. This book can be one element of support for you. Use the Creative CORE Method to bring yourself to a new level of engagement, consciousness, intentionality, and action as you move towards whatever your vision is.

Motivation

Sometimes maintaining motivation is a challenge. You can feel like there is no flow. You can find yourself resistant or just plain afraid and stuck. It can be hard to keep moving forward and disheartening to find yourself returning to the same problem. That experience can undermine your confidence and certainty. All these elements combined may stop you in your tracks if you are not prepared and mindful. It is bound to happen and that is why it has been mentioned several different ways that **you need support in place to help keep you going.**

I'll let you in on a secret here, and I speak from firsthand experience. Writing this book has been an embodiment of all those struggles. I have had to rely on a lot of external support. I have used Zoom coworking calls with a willing partner over the course of many, many days. I would say 40% of the time I was away from the computer, eating, walking the dog, staring out into space and just generally feeling anxious and doubting the book. I persisted because I wanted to finish this project. I invested in three different, not inexpensive, coaching programs and spent 6 years in this process. As I write my head imagines the Reader thinking "and this is all you came up with?" And my answer would have to be yes. This project was the outcome of my CORE vision. I wanted to do something unique to me and the R recipe I roughed out included teaching my own curriculum so the Execute step, where the rubber meets the road, had write a book on the list.

While thinking skills are half of the toolkit, doing is the other half; your mindset and the support you enlist are elements that will get you through to the goal.

The process worked for me. I experienced all the aspects: going forward, backward, zooming-in, zooming-out, refocusing, starting over, putting in work and taking it out, rearranging, listening to feedback. The piece that kept me going was my original "C," the communication with self that said: I want to help others improve their relationship with creativity. I needed to share my version of this message in case someone needed to hear it the way I say it.

Time and Progress are NOT Linear

I think it's important to mention that while writing and talking about the CORE process, it might sound linear. You do move forward through the steps, but it is not always a straight line. Have you ever experienced a learning curve or felt the frustration of going forward, thinking you've gotten somewhere but the next time you try it you've fallen backwards? Have you had the experience of making a goal and getting off course, then having to reset and course-correct?

As you progress and encounter moments when you feel stalled, it is important that you acknowledge yourself for the progress and process you have made. The trajectory can remain forward, but day-to-day you may not always see it that way. How you deal with the ups-and-downs of your ongoing process can have profound consequences on your outcome.

Your experience can run the gamut of seeing something exciting evolve, flourish, and go out into the world, or you can get frustrated, choosing to throw in the towel and walk away. Much depends on your perseverance and willingness to keep going despite challenges and delays. You know what kind of person you are. If you are one who chooses to stop and quit, maybe it's time to decide to have a different experience.

Gather your support network of friends and advisors you trust, take your self-care seriously, and be patient with yourself while you work on your plan of action. If you don't have these things in place, perhaps that in and of itself is a challenge for you to work on first. How might you develop supportive friends, better self-care, or more patience so you can move forward through the change you intended to create?

Making something from nothing and asking others to go along with you is an act of courage and leap of faith. It is an amazing gift that we humans get to experience.

Be gentle. When bumps in the road occur, be cautious about judging, condemning, or blaming yourself (or others). That type of self-talk is a kind of defense against disappointment for many people; left unchecked it can also lead to the path that justifies quitting. Instead, take time to reflect, assess and consider what other help or direction you might need.

As a coach, it is important to me to hold your vision while being a cheerleader and support for the process.

By mastering the Creative CORE Method, you will be able to take a step back and remind yourself that as a creator, you're collaborating with all of life. If that notion is hard to imagine, you can try a meditation:

Consider all that had to happen for you to be right where you are at this very moment, reading this very book. There are resources that you recognize and those that you don't, yet it all conspired to get you here. Imagine there are just as many if not more resources ready and available to help you get to the next phase if you just put yourself forth.

As you sit here, use your mind to feel your body. Do you end at the edge of your flesh? Can you feel beyond? Try imagining that you're filling the space you are in. Going beyond that, the energy is much larger and your pull and your reach are beyond. Your connections and life intersections are all part of the Web of Life you are a part of. Imagine extending into all of that power and resource. That is what I mean when I say you are collaborating with ALL OF LIFE.

Creativity is Life and Life is Creative

My perspective is this: I think about creativity and I think about life. I look out at the natural world and see the myriad of forms and think that is creativity, that is life. There is no evidence of one without the other.

An activity I use as a warm-up in Evolutionary Improv is to walk around slowly and notice that you take up space. You can stretch your arms and be as big as you can possibly make yourself; you are free to take up space. Breathe; notice you can breathe as much as you need. You can move in any way your body can move. If you can do that, you can feel that you are alive. While you're alive in this world you have the capacity to create. You can think, do, speak, act. You have as much permission as anybody else. Life is life. It is everywhere, it is abundant, available and yours.

Dealing with resistance?

Resistance is a phenomenon of not doing the thing you say you want to do. Writer's block, procrastination, fear, terror, laziness, "something came up" and "I just didn't have time." It's all part of it. Books have been written about resistance. Coaches will say your vision isn't big enough and to get back in touch with your "why." Make goals, keep them... and it's all good advice. But sometimes you just feel like you're filled with lead. Sometimes it lasts a long time, sometimes it passes, and sometimes you just have to do what little you can in spite of it. Ultimately the only way through, is through. I think the biggest challenge is how to love and forgive yourself along the way. Different people have different temperaments. Do you know what works for you? Do you need to be around people? Do you like to work alone? Will setting goals and working with a coach for accountability help you succeed? Will putting money on the line and paying for support make the difference? Will telling everybody you know what you're up to work for you? At different times in your process, you will need different aids to keep you going. It's not a one-size-fits-all, but you certainly have tools in your arsenal that keep you going and feeling alive.

Instead of trying to avoid resistance can you use it?

Can you bring your resistance and express it? Can you bring anger, annoyance, joy, fear... and somehow imagine incorporating them into the process and getting present with and dancing with the feelings while you learn? What can your resistance tell you about yourself?

While I was on a call the other day, the presenter was sharing an experience about signing up for a race and hitting a wall. She really wanted to quit training but had already worked herself up to running a significant amount of mileage.

She was really struggling with her commitment to run the race. One afternoon, she forced herself to get on the treadmill and imagined herself painting a painting with the feelings she was having as she ran. Suddenly, the experience was not just getting through the mileage, but rather what she was creating in her mind and the feelings she was processing going through the miles.

This was such an extraordinary experience for her that she had a breakthrough about how she could use her resistance to fuel the very thing she was resisting, while also processing feelings and using her imagination at the same time.

Sometimes we have to play games in our heads to keep going.

When you are really up against it, remember to invite the unexpected into your process. If you're having a down day or feeling really stuck, give yourself a timeout and do something, go somewhere, or call somebody that is not in your normal sphere. Declare that you're looking for answers, support, or insights and then keep your mind open.

Make room for the unexpected

It is so much fun when little gifts you could not have imagined get placed in your path. If you need a little boost of confidence or energy, and you started the synchronicity journal I talked about in Chapter 2, have a look at that, and remind yourself of the small things that went right when you least expected it.

One of my favorite stories from my journal is the time I had been selected to offer my Evolutionary Improv class at the Pittsburgh Comedy Festival. It was my first time delivering that class in an environment like that. I flew across the country, planned my class beautifully, and realized I could really use a Bluetooth speaker because music is integral to the class. I was very stressed out by not having one and at the time they were not as readily available inexpensively as they are today. I didn't want to lay out the cash and figured I'd have to just use my phone speaker and deal with it. Meanwhile, the night before my class I went out to dinner with an LA friend's mother who lived in Pittsburgh. She brought along a friend, and he suggested I check out an art fair not far from where I was staying the morning before my class. I thought that would be fun, so I went. One exhibitor was the company Xfinity. They had a big rig set up with interactive demos so you could experience the quality of their internet and high definition. I went in and tried out the Virtual Reality demo. As a thank you for stopping in they offered a choice of promotional gifts. One of the gift options was a Bluetooth speaker. I couldn't believe my eyes. I took the speaker and sailed out of there high on feelings of delight, surprise, and gratitude. I approached my class with a little extra pep in my step, feeling like the Universe had my back. There I was, somewhere I never planned to be. Just by saying yes and showing up, I allowed myself the experience of a prayer being answered. It was just such a positive fist-bump from the Universe. Life was looking out for me.

Now that you have the mindset piece and know that you are not alone in this creative endeavor, it's time to start your process and embark on your Creative CORE experience.

Chapter 8.

Introduction to

Using your Creative CORE

Throughout the experience of your creative process, you will be in dialogue with yourself. I will ask you questions to ask yourself. I do this because curiosity is an integral mindset for creativity. An aspect of the nature of creativity is that in its early phases, it is open-ended. Developing a habit of asking yourself exploratory questions helps invite research, contemplation, collaboration, and inventiveness. This mindset will help drive you through the whole C-O-R-E process.

Now that you understand the general approach, I will provide steps with some accompanying tools and processes to support your thinking. As you engage with the steps and tools to identify a problem of your own, then creativity as a process will make sense. This book is a guide to navigating the Creative CORE Method, which offers you an approach to experiencing the transformative power of creativity in your life.

How do I know creativity is the best problem-solving tool to use?

When you find yourself in a situation where you feel stuck, and the way through is not obvious (or for some reason you just don't feel motivated), you have a good starting point for using the Creative CORE. You may have a sense of what needs to be done, you may even be saying to yourself you know the answer. However, if you just can't get started, you may benefit from a tweak in your thinking to refresh your motivation.

Working through your problem using the structure of the Creative CORE can liberate new energy and enthusiasm. You can overcome feeling stuck by discovering new perspectives of how you view your current challenge. The new insights can give you the juice you need to start moving forward. If you feel resistant, reframing the situation can provide a breakthrough that alters your feelings and allows you to see your circumstances a bit differently so that you feel empowered to take action.

Sometimes I work with people who insist that they know what the problem is. I guide them through the process anyway because its purpose is to shift perspective. Even a little adjustment and redirection provides an opening. Becoming able to see an old problem in a new way liberates energy and reduces some of the hold the situation has on the psyche. It's like taking your power back.

If you are just not open, then it may not be the right problem for you to focus on at this time. Pick another area of your life where you feel stuck or want to see a change. For example, I recently worked with a woman who was sure her block was money and how to make more of it. Once we started talking, however, it was actually about managing her time more effectively. Another example comes from a friend who was compulsively dating and becoming very depressed by it. She insisted she did not like being on her own, but upon reflection, security was the real issue. Once she got clear on that, she started to focus on how she did have control to create more feelings of security in her life.

Messages from within telling you it's time to Engage Your Creativity

If you have felt any of these feelings, or heard yourself say these or similar words, then a creative solution could offer you a breakthrough.

Read the following statements and put a check mark to the ones that ring true or feel familiar.

"I know what I need to do but I just don't feel like doing it."

"I know what I should do but I just don't do it."

"I know what I want to have happen, but I don't know what to do first/next."

"I see the end result; I just don't know how to get there."

"I am not getting the results I want."

"I want to have a different experience."

"It just feels like a big mess, and I don't know what to do next."

"I don't know where to start."

"I don't know what I want."

"I feel like I'm wasting my life away."

"I want to do or experience X and I don't even know

what that means."

Did you put check marks next to any of the phrases?

Review your check marked comments and ask yourself: Is there a solution I can apply that's readily available? Do I know what to do next?

If there is not a readily available solution, then you have identified a gap. Your desire to bridge that gap is your invitation to apply creative thinking.

Make a note about that gap:

_____

_____

_____

This gap you just identified could be a place for you to try the CORE process in your own life. Would it be worthwhile to delve into this area and discover what you can create as a solution?

In case you are thinking it's not a great area, I want to give you a few questions so you can differentiate when creativity may not be the solution. You may just need to pay someone for help, or the motivation may truly not be there at this time. Here are a few elements to consider.

When don't you need the creative process:

1. It's not your problem, and you have not been asked to fix it (unless you're an entrepreneur looking for a problem to solve and are intent on building a business solution around that problem you fix).

2. Solutions exist, and you can pay someone to do it for you. Paying for help may end up being part of the creative solution you come up with to close the gap or the problem you identified. 3. You are really and truly not motivated at this time. You're allowed to choose not to do something. Liberate your energy by taking it off your to-do list and get living.

Assuming you still have a problem you would like to apply creative thinking to, the next chapter will take you into the first steps in depth. There are questions and worksheets so you can guide yourself through the process of communicating with self, the C in CORE.

Chapter 9:

Step 1: COMMUNICATION WITH SELF

Your desire expressed - The first step of the CORE process is COMMUNICATION WITH SELF.

This might sound odd, but think about it. If you're going to be leading yourself into change, the ability and willingness to hear your trusted inner voice clearly is imperative. You need to have the presence of mind to receive and process the communication from yourself that change is needed. Whether you call it a desire or a vision, the "I want", or "I need" has to be communicated and received by you so you can ignite the inner pilot light that will illuminate and power-up your next steps.

TOOLS/MINDSET

Intimacy with self

To begin with, the Creative CORE process relies on intimacy with self. My definition of intimacy with self, in terms of the creative process, is listening and being curious and open to receive and document your inner musing. A mindset of acceptance must be adopted. Become willing to hear yourself and receive the desires that are communicated. Desires take the forms of what you want and what you want to let go of. As you practice this process, just listen, document, and accept. Avoid resistance. At this point you're only putting words on a page, documenting your inner musings coming forth.

Holding Space

Holding space means carving out time and creating an environment that allows you to relax so that your mind can open. and you can connect and listen to your inner voice. Think of creating an environment of intimacy with yourself. Depending on what you like, this can include lighting a candle, putting on music that helps you relax and focus, possibly a warm beverage, maybe you like to soak in a warm bath. As they say, you do you. Just take action to support your mind and body in feeling safe and relaxed so you can be honest with yourself.

If this is a challenge for you, imagine holding space for yourself like you would a dear friend or child. Give yourself the best patient, non-judgmental listening you can muster. It is in these moments of reflective communion that you can take stock of your life and start to ask yourself questions that provide clarity and reflection.

The supporting mindsets for this inquiry are acceptance and allowing. Treat yourself with kindness. If you feel uncertain, imagine how a therapist would hold space for you. You can also invite a trusted friend to read you the questions provided later in this chapter as you write. Sharing what you write is not necessary. This is an exercise for your own personal exploration.

Pro Tip: you can record the questions and play them to yourself.

Depending on the urgency of your situation, you may experience your internal communication as a whisper that calls, or it may be a pleading voice telling you something's got to give because you just don't want whatever this is anymore. You might experience it as a bottoming out, or burnout. Some symptoms of that type of burnout are feeling like "I don't care how much money they pay me; I just don't care anymore." "I'd rather put a stick in my eye than have one more day of…" or "I just know this isn't healthy for me." You may have uttered the phrase "I want this thing and I don't even know what it means."

Maybe you don't want to wait until it gets that extreme, maybe you are experiencing general dissatisfaction, a belief that "I can do better." Whatever it is for you, that internal communication needs to be acknowledged before you start. It's your impetus, your push towards the cliff of intentional change. Are you ready to stop pushing it aside? Once you say "yes, I am," you have reached the starting point for exploration.

The first step is to clarify your vision. What is it that you want for yourself? What is it that you wish for? You will gather data about your present circumstances and state of mind by answering the following questions for yourself. You can use the prompts below to start to see and hear what you are communicating.

COMMUNICATION WITH SELF Phase 1: Generate Your Vision

You can use the prompts below as sentence starters:

I wish that _____

_____

_____.

It would be great if_____

_____

_____.

What I am yearning to experience is: _____

_____

_____.

I want to be/do/have: _____

_____

_____.

COMMUNICATION WITH SELF Phase 2:
Uncover what's in the way?

This is a series of reflective questions to help you illuminate and codify some elements that might be contained in your vision.

I feel too much _____.
I don't feel enough _____.

I have too much _____.
I don't have enough _____.

I hear too much _____.
I don't hear enough _____.

I don't like _____.
I like _____.

I could live without _____.
I can't live without _____.

I spend too much time doing _____.
I don't do enough _____.

I've already accomplished _____

I want to accomplish _____.

I'm so tired of _____.
I'd like a new experience around _____.

Something I always wanted to try is_____.

If I could just change _____
_____, everything would be different.

I don't want to die without ever having _____.

A cause or organization I'd really like to support is

_____.

Imagining myself looking back a year from now I would smile if I saw that I had done/achieved/let go of this

_____.

Review what you wrote. Write down words that repeat.

_____

Do you see any blocks or impediments that repeat?

_____

Do you recognize a theme running through?

_____

If you have trouble identifying a theme, see if one of the sentence starters below ignites your thinking.

- A thread I notice is_____.

- I am noticing feelings of_____.

- I have a desire for_____.

- A pattern I am seeing is_____.

- What it all comes down to is_____.

- When all is said and done, what's left is_____.

- If I could sum up what I am seeing in one word, it would be_____.

It is very common to approach this phase thinking you already know what your problem is. You will know you've fallen for it if you hear yourself say "oh, I already know what it is, it's always..." "I know, if I just focused on ... I would be fine." However, I have seen over and over again that it is very important to approach this theme finding process with an open and curious mind.

Allow yourself to be surprised and discover nuance. Even a slight tweak at how you look at a situation can open an unexpected door in your thinking, which in turn liberates new and motivating energy. This is a creative process. You're looking for solutions you don't know yet, so be willing to rephrase your problem so that it, too, feels new.

If you just can't bring yourself to look at it differently, note the way you see it today. Physically write it down so you don't have to worry about holding it in memory. Use this spot here to capture it the way you see it today. Doing this will free you up; just for exploration, see what you come up with as you try to look at the problem with a fresh take.

_____

_____

COMMUNICATION WITH SELF Phase 3: Pulling it together: Review what you wrote, put a checkmark beside or highlight the most resonant and important words.

Consider the following questions as you review:

- What ideas are important?
- Where do I have influence?
- Do any of these require new thinking to be achieved?

Write down what you see or learned about your communications with self.

_____

_____

_____

OUTCOME: Combining information into a concise statement of a goal or wish.

1) What I see is that currently, I _____

_____

2) But what I'd really like to be/do/have/wish for instead is _____

_____

Review the two statements and come up with a concise, forward-looking vision of what you want even if you don't know what it means.

Write your vision statement here:

_____

_____

_____

Now that you have communicated to yourself a clarified vision statement of desire, it is time to turn it into a question that will catapult you into the next stage of the process – OPENING TO IDEAS.

COMMUNICATION WITH SELF Phase 4: Using one of the three statement starters below, turn your vision statement into a question that causes you to generate ideas.

Using one of these three options:

1) How might I + vision statement

2) How to + vision statement

3) What might be all the ways I + Vision statement

Write your vision statement as a question_____

_____?

Examples: of how a broad vision combined with a statement starter becomes a catapult for OPENING TO IDEAS.

Let's revisit the real-life examples from earlier in the book:

Vivian:

Vision: I want to do something unique to me and have creativity be at the center of my life.

Catapult question: How might I do something completely unique and have creativity be at the center of my life?

(Next step preview) I wonder if there is such a thing as a graduate program in Creativity.

Kristen:

Vision: I want to work with African Women

Catapult question: In what ways might I work with African Women?

(Next step preview) What if I went to Africa, met women, and just listened?

Susan:

Vision: I want to quit nursing and have a Goat Farm

Catapult question: What might be all the ways I can quit nursing and have a goat farm?

(Next step preview) Maybe I can find somewhere else that has goats and start spending time supporting them.

Mike:

Vision: To find healing by connecting with myself at all ages.

Catapult question: What might be a way to reconnect with myself and revisit some of the tough years?

(Next step preview) What if as an experiment, I find and spend time with a person at every age 1-40 to interview and observe?

Debbie:

Vision: To be prepared in case my government contract goes away

Catapult question: "What might be all the ways I can

become more visible outside of the government and travel more."

(Next step preview) Debbie started wanting abundance, ease, peace of mind in her financial life and workflow. She kept focusing on the money and the work as the solutions but used the words "ease" and "peace of mind" consistently. I suggested that she focus on the ease and peace of mind because they were so persistent in her communication. She was just not accustomed to having that be the driver because the money and workflow were her priorities, and out of habit she focused on them. By gently suggesting that she simply create her vision about peace of mind and ease, she could open herself to new concepts around that. Her question became focused around "what I'd really like is a feeling of ease and peace of mind (about money and workflow). What might be all the ways I could experience ease and peace of mind on a daily basis?" This question catapulted her into the next phase– OPENING TO IDEAS...

Note: A friend whom I sent the chapter to wrote back that she was in a funk so didn't do it. I countered that it's the perfect time to do it. If the funk is regarding something persistent, then new thinking could be just the solution to help move through it.

Chapter 10:

Step 2: OPENING TO IDEAS

EXPLORE AND ANALYZE

The **O** in CORE stands for **OPENING TO IDEAS**. Once you have communicated a vision to yourself and formulated a juicy question out of it (like you did in the previous step), your brain will automatically start thinking of ways to answer the question. That drive indicates that you're primed to open to ideas. You may be familiar with the concept of brainstorming, and that is exactly what it is time for. You are entering a generative phase. The technical term is divergent thinking. That is when you allow your train of thought to go off the rails in many directions. For a writer, the analogy would be the rough draft, where you just get everything onto the page without editing or criticizing.

The process you are entering now is to generate ideas, not to craft the final solution– remember this is only the second step, the O of The Creative CORE Method.

Tools/Mindset

This phase has you answering the questions and imagining multiple ways you might answer them. The mindset is to allow yourself to generate ideas in a free-flowing manner. Use your imagination broadly, even impractically. Have you ever had a great laugh with someone where you riff off one another, building a scenario that may be ridiculous but you keep topping each other and adding to the conversation? When I was thirteen my best friend Cynthia and I were in a food court at the mall, and in conversation we came up with the ridiculous idea (for the time) of cars driving themselves. We laughed as we imagined how they would brake and change lanes, park, and do all the things a driver would do. We laughed so hard and had so much fun in that conversation that it still makes me look back and smile. Look at cars today. If only we were inventors. The point is that what we were doing was diverging, brainstorming, playing and building on ideas. We didn't edit or consider all the ways it wasn't possible while we were in the process. I invite you to allow for whimsy, far-fetched, silly, or impossible ideas. The reason is that something ridiculous can spark something not ridiculous. You may discover a seed which can be planted. You may be firing neurons you don't normally fire. But they may connect with another where a connection has never been made and then you find yourself coming up with something totally unexpected that excites and inspires you. Keep the critic out of this process. Rather, keep it light but push yourself a little further than you think you can go.

Capture your ideas. Write them down on Post-its and put them on the wall, say them out loud into a recorder, draw them, or have a friend take dictation. Just make sure to keep a record so you can refer to them later if needed.

While you are in this generative phase, stretch yourself to consider all the possibilities you can think of. It Is recommended to try for at least 35 ideas.

Mental games you can play include things like taking cues from nature, noticing how nature solves a problem and thinking how that could relate to your question.

Think through the lens of someone you know and how they might answer the question

How about someone younger or older than you?

You can use the OPENING TO IDEAS worksheet to support your process.

OPENING TO IDEAS: Phase 1: Carry forward your clear, open-ended question from the previous phase.

Write your vision question from the previous section here:

_____

Example questions: How might I change the way I work so I can travel more? Or What might be all the ways to reinvent my social life so that it's more fulfilling?

Phrase your question so that it activates you and catapults you into thinking of ways you can answer it.

This phase is the time to immerse yourself in possibility. Curiously consider all the ways to answer your question. You can do this alone, or with someone else whose mind you like and trust. Depending on the nature of the question, you might ask friends, family, or even an expert to help you develop a nuanced understanding of the problem.

Inviting others to help you answer the question allows other perspectives that are unburdened by your potentially innate biases of what can or can't be done. Explain to them that you're just generating ideas of all sorts right now and capturing them. They are not solving your problem just coming up with ideas with hopes that something they may contribute to your process.

During this generative stage, tell all the practical, editorial voices to wait their turn. They'll work their magic in the next step. For now, allow yourself to play. It's an idea party and all guests are welcome.

Following are a few mindset rules that increase the effectiveness of this generating stage.

The mindset is as follows:

* Reach for many ideas, with a goal of 30 or 50

* Piggyback on ideas. If one thought sparks another, use that too.

* Don't edit. If another idea comes up alongside or better, write it on a new line or Post-it.

* Go a little wild!

Pro-tip: Use external sources to help you generate ideas.

* Photos: pick up a magazine and scroll through images. Ask yourself, "When I look at this image through the lens of my question, what ideas emerge?"

* You can go for a walk, taking time to notice things in your surroundings, and pose the same question while you're walking. If an idea bubbles up, be sure to capture it.

* Ask yourself from the perspective of a dog, an alien, a boss, a child, a partner, or anyone you respect: what ideas might they see?

* Capture your ideas, writing them individually on Post-its. Or, while you're walking, you can talk into a recorder. Or stop and write them down.

* Once you have exhausted the possibilities for answering your question, take a break and get ready for phase two.

Make it fun. As an improvisation teacher, I see that even in an environment where it's all made up, people still struggle to overcome the conditioning that says there is a right thing to say or do. In this practice, allow your ideas to go broad. Try selecting a numerical number of ideas as a goal and push yourself, even with nonsensical ideas, to reach the goal. At some point you're just going to have to write down ridiculous things. As you allow yourself to write those ridiculous things, something not so ridiculous will emerge. Push yourself to persevere and stretch so you can keep generating ideas.

It is helpful to not put too much stock in any one idea because there is a whole process that follows. It will help you refine and shape whatever ideas you choose for moving forward.

Make it a goal to surprise yourself with your own untapped reserves.

Once you have finished generating ideas to answer the question you have completed phase one. Congratulations!

OPENING TO IDEAS Phase 2: Sift, sort, rank and reconfigure.

Tools you need: markers, stickers, and a space to put your Post-its on the wall (if you haven't already)

Here's where you get to edit and judge.

This is an organizational step. You did the work of diverging when you came up with your ideas; now it's time to shift gears and sit in the editor and arranger seat. You will be sifting, sorting and regrouping.

Mindset focus: Keeping your vision question as the focus, review your ideas. You'll be looking for ideas that spark possibility.

Look through what you have written and put a mark or a sticker on the ones that light you up. We'll call them hits.

So first sort the hits from the neutrals or duds.

When you have them separated out:

1) Look for themes and group the ones that are thematically similar together.

2) Paraphrase the theme as you see it. What action does it represent?

3) Any standouts you just like, because they feel right.

Write the themes as an action (ex. reaching, opening, meeting, starting, stopping, learning, hiring, buying, selling, etc.).

OPENING TO IDEAS: Phase 3: Drafting an idea statement

Gather the elements and formulate a one-sentence active vision.

Now it is time to consolidate and rephrase the ideas you selected to bring forward. Review what you came up with in terms of actions and themes.

What you will be generating next is a preliminary plan of action that reads like a sentence. Start it using the following phrase:

What I see myself doing is...

First: Look for themes. Are there some that are thematically similar? If so, group them. Use Post-its and put them in an area together.

Second: Are there some that are just plain standouts? Keep them.

Third: Are there some that are a little out there but have a glimmer of possibility that might make sense if you modified them?

Fourth: Are there some that are just no's? Put them aside.

Once you have grouped them as such, look for themes.

How can the themes be phrased as an action?

Can you form it all into a workable idea that answers the prompt:

What I see myself doing is...

OPENING TO IDEAS: Phase 4: Convergent Idea Selection: Weed out and consolidate

What you just completed was the divergent phase of the OPENING TO IDEAS phase of the Creative CORE Method process. Next, we will take those ideas and apply a critical eye to them.

In the same way that Diverging has mindsets that improve output, so does the Convergent phase. Those principles are:

- Discernment with a touch of possibility

- Keeping a wildcard in the mix if it sparks something

- Keeping your vision as your north star

What this is essentially saying is that now is the time to prune and edit your ideas but keep an eye toward newness. Discernment with a touch of possibility allows you to say no when it's right, but also keep a little question mark at times when something isn't exactly a yes and not exactly a no. You may not know for sure how it fits, or whether it will, but if there's something there, just keep it for now. Maintain the attitude of possibility, and temper with real questions about how it may or may not develop into a workable solution.

Pro-tip: Keeping a wildcard or novel idea in the mix can elevate and stretch your thinking, because a wild idea you like may cause your brain to make an unexpected connection.

If you like editing or saying no, this will be your fun time. Imagine putting on a gold miner's helmet because you're going to be digging, excavating, and finding the golden nuggets.

It's time to review all the ideas you came up with and apply a combination of discernment and imagination. This is a balancing act of keeping where you want to go in mind, looking through the ideas, and seeing which ones spark you (and seem workable) while also finding the wildcards.

Seek riches below the surface, looking for clues. Invite your intuition.

Questions to keep in mind as you review

Does it have a seed of possibility that is in alignment with my objectives?

Do any of the ideas have a sparkly quality?

Does it excite you?

Does something resonate deeply?

Put a check mark beside ideas you like or if you used Post-Its, physically group the ones you selected next each other. You are sifting and sorting at this point.

If you are a very practical person, you may just want to default to what you think you know will or won't work because you can see down the road. Allow yourself this gift of not seeing down the road. Pick ideas that speak to you at the heart, gut, or even humor level.

Remember, this is about a creative solution and by definition that means it does not exist yet. Be in the discovery.

If you keep your Clarified Vision as the outcome you are aiming for, the rest of the pieces will line up.

Keep your objective in mind while attempting to pull together elements that will be developed into the recipe that will help you cook up the plan of action that takes you into the experience you desire.

Managing your energy

This type of work, if it's new and you've given it all you got, requires real energy. If you feel you need to rest between these steps, do so. At this juncture you'll be switching mental gears. Go eat, take a walk, reflect on how you feel and check in with yourself. Are you excited with the work you've done so far? Have any insights come forth?

OPENING TO IDEAS: Phase 5: Sift, sort, select

Review your ideas again.

Look for ones that are similar or complement each other.

Group similar ideas together.

Once grouped, notice: Do the clusters have a theme? Write that down.

As you are doing this clustering and finding themes, you may become aware that individual ideas or clusters can be strung together to form a loose plan of action.

Outcome: A preliminary action plan

String together the ideas you came up with into a preliminary action plan.

The phrase you'll build on is: **What I see myself doing is...**

Complete the phrase with the ideas you just selected. This is a first draft so it does not have to be perfect. It is just a way to contain and order the ideas so you can see how they might make sense working together.

Example from a student: What I see myself doing is finally letting go of my apartment in New York. I will sell it, put the money towards buying a mid-century fixer-upper in Los Angeles. I'll learn about remodeling, develop my expertise of mid-century aesthetics, and blog about the process.

Generally, you want to limit to 3-5 of your ideas.

Write your initial action plan here:

What I see myself doing is:

_____

_____

_____

This is the completion of the **O-Opening to Ideas** phase. Next you will take that preliminary plan of action and move into the **R-Rough Out Your Recipe** phase where you will tweak and further refine it so that you emerge with an actual plan that will give you a clear path to move forward towards **E-Executing Your Plan**.

Good work. Are you noticing possibilities now? Do you feel energized by what has emerged thus far?

Chapter 11:

Step 3: ROUGH OUT YOUR RECIPE

TWEAK/TAILOR & IMPROVE

Welcome to the next step of your creative CORE journey. You have arrived at **R** This is the phase where you take your discrete ideas and build them into actual recipe you can follow.

You'll begin by reviewing and considering your "what I see myself doing" statement that you came up with in the previous section. You'll notice what is good about it, ask yourself about the possibilities it might open, and finally, what challenges you see. Once again, you will be using your brainstorming skills to consider how to overcome the biggest challenges you identify. Then you will hone again and finally create a robust recipe you can follow.

This developmental phase can feel like drudgery for some people, while others love this process and can get stuck in questioning all the minutiae.

If you're someone for whom this feels like drudgery and are tempted to skip this section, please don't. As with all phases of the process, unexpected insights can be revealed. Try making it fun or challenging by giving yourself a timed session in which to answer the questions that appear in the next section. Five to ten minutes should put adequate pressure on you to move quickly and let yourself know that it is a limited process. You can reward yourself with a dance break or treat or whatever else makes you feel alive and acknowledged. You can also recruit a friend or family member and ask them to read the questions to you and sit with you while you answer the questions. Sometimes the presence of another person in the room (or on a camera) is all you need. Being asked the questions also engages your auditory sense, which may trigger you differently than reading.

The purpose of this phase is to refine your next steps and consider important elements, such as what help you might need, who might help you, and what order you might get things done and when.

The benefits of taking on this step thoroughly include: starting to think in terms of step-by-step plans; making some things time-bound; and making sure that your goals are realistic and attainable. You can start embracing your ideas as real possibilities by talking about them with the people whom you will be helping or need help from.

ROUGH OUT YOUR RECIPE

The R in CORE: ROUGH OUT YOUR RECIPE

OUTCOME OF R: A roughed-out recipe that reads like a step-by-step action plan.

If you think of a recipe, it has ingredients and instructions. That is what you will create for yourself here. The ideas are the ingredients and the actions are the instructions. What you have brought forward from your work in the previous sections is a set of ideas that seem workable and give you a sense of excitement, possibility, and motivation. Those ideas are the ingredients of the recipe you will cook up to deliver you to your vision.

Are you excited by what you see? Is it causing little fireworks to go off, like little flashes of light and insight that give you that chomping-at-the-bit sensation of wanting to get on with it? If so, you're in the right place.

ROUGH OUT YOUR RECIPE Phase 1: Refine and develop your recipe:

Just as before, you will sift and sort in order to further refine what you came up with. This will help you see it as a manageable, clear, and real tool.

1) Rewrite your "What I see myself doing" statement here:

———————————————————————————————————

Review your plan and ask yourself the following questions. Answer according to how the plan reads now.

1a) This is good as it is because

———————————————————————————————————

1b) I am excited about how this will or how this might

———————————————————————————————————

2) Possibilities I can see that it might cause/generate/open up

———————————————————————————————————

2a) What if it causes/generates/opens up

————————————————————————————————————

3) Elements that give me pause; I can't see how I might

————————————————————————————————————

3a) I don't know how to

————————————————————————————————————

3b) I am concerned that

————————————————————————————————————

Review what you came up with.

Section 3 are all forms of concerns that if left unattended could stop your progress. Take time now to review what you wrote. Circle the most relevant and challenging ones. Then, on a clean sheet of paper, write the concern at the top and ask yourself "How do I overcome it?" Start to brainstorm a list of ways. Do this for each individual concern that could really derail you if not handled.

How to overcome (concern)?

Do this for the most pressing concerns you came up with.

When you feel you have thoroughly thought about solutions for the primary concerns you selected, it's time to sift and sort again.

Generating your new recipe

Review your original "what I see myself doing" statement.

Review your answers to the questions above.

Review the best answers to your concerns and questions.

It is a lot of data and ideas.

Start to crystalize and formulate a modified and more specific statement that begins with, **What I now see myself doing is...** Incorporate the solutions to concerns as well as any of the possibilities you just wrote above. It may seem long but don't worry; include details that have solutions, actions, dates, outcomes– you're really creating something broad and deep here.

Example:

Patricia: "What I now see myself doing is becoming visible to a wider audience by reaching out to professional societies to present to fellow ADR professionals the merits of our work with potential clients. I also see myself writing a book for those faced with deciding between litigation and mediation, as well as contributing to online journals, professional magazines and possibly creating a blog.

Broken up another way to write your new recipe is:

The plan I now see for myself goes like this

———————————————————————————————————

———————————————————————————————————

———————————————————————————————————

The actions I now see myself taking are these

_____

_____

_____

The people I will contact are

_____

_____

_____

The first steps are

_____

_____

_____

I will do _____

_____

by_____

_____

Conclusion

You have reached the end of the R step. Congratulations! You have now roughed out your recipe for action; your solution will be carried forward into the EXECUTE YOUR PLAN stage. What you came up with I hope feels new, energizing and aligned with your vision. You should be able to see a pathway forward.

What comes next is the **EXECUTING YOUR PLAN** step. It's the time for the rubber to meet the road. In your recipe, there ought to be people, groups or resources included that can support you along the way. Some people are great Executors and are just chomping at the bit to get things going. Others are more tentative or cautious. You probably know where you fall- I hope you have the wherewithal to find support and ask questions, so you don't get stuck in uncertainty. You have just done a lot of work on your own behalf. The solution you have in your hand is evidence that the creative process took place. You used your creativity to generate something remarkable and life changing for yourself. Allow it to thrive, get the help, stick to the dates, review your vision, and stay motivated.

On to the **E** of The Creative CORE Method...

Chapter 12:

Step 4: EXECUTING YOUR PLAN

Emerging Activity: VALIDATE & EXECUTE

This phase is where you start to enact the elements of your plan. It is going from broad strokes to specific tangible activities that you organize into a specific, executable plan. You've arrived here with a robust and roughed out plan and now you need to break it down into executable steps that will build on one another.

Embark on your Roadmap

Step 4: Execution (Implementation) stage: Creating a plan of action.

The outcome of the stage you just completed is a robust recipe, a **draft solution** generated using your creative thinking processes. It should be encoded with your vision, and therefore have a greater likelihood that by continuing to refine and follow the steps (which you are about to outline), you will be driving yourself towards the fulfillment of your vision and away from the current status quo.

The nature of a creative solution is that it transforms your situation. I hope you are seeing something unexpected taking shape, like a shimmery new portal you can see yourself walking towards and through. You may now find in yourself a new willingness to act differently. You may notice that choices that once seemed unthinkable are suddenly feeling like the right solution And before you know it, you're executing your plan.

EXECUTING YOUR PLAN Phase 1: Executing your plan

This is the place where the rubber starts to meet the road, but first you must have steps to follow. Like the preceding phases of the CORE process, there are two phases of the Executing step.

You must mentally prepare yourself for challenges as you start to consider how to turn your (recipe) solution into an executable plan. You can think like a reporter and ask questions.

- What order will actions be taken?
- Who will do a specific task?
- What will you/they do?
- When will it be done?

This might feel overwhelming as you read this. If so, I can totally relate. The truth is, if you have gotten to this point, you have a feel for the many steps and actions. This is just asking you to order them in a way that makes sense, put some goal times for completion, assign the actions you can to others, and just generally bring the data into a workable and actionable form so that you are empowered.

Phase 1 asks you to read the solution (review the recipe) you created. Begin imagining your preparation and the process you have lined up for yourself. As you do, ask yourself: who or what is going to be on your side, supporting you and going with your flow? Who and what will be assisting you? Write them down, so you have a list.

As you clarify these questions, a new level of insight and ideas may start to form, allowing you to refine your recipe to include steps that consider how you will work with others and bring them in, or not.

While this happens, you may start to see phases naturally occurring. You can use different colored pens to separate the phases and organize your thoughts.

As you move forward in action, each new activity will blossom, and you will likely find you need to keep relying on the elements of the CORE process.

If you are faced with a situation that requires more solutions, use a statement starter to create a question to diverge on.

If you are faced with many choices, try sifting and sorting and select the best ideas or options.

Here are some questions that might be helpful. You may want to skimp on spending time answering some of these questions, but down the line, having these things in place will help you when resistance comes up or you are facing challenges to moving forward. Front load your work as much as possible so that you are prepared when obstacles emerge, you get tired, or you are questioning everything. Those feelings are all normal parts of the experience. Knowing this, you can have the presence of mind–when thoughts that might derail you emerge–to say to yourself: this is resistance, fear, or is overwhelming and it is part of the process.

You can proactively bolster yourself by putting supports in place to keep you on track mentally, and emotionally. Take some time to think forward.

You can use the questions below to trigger ideas about who, or what, might be nice to have in place before any powerful negative feelings arise that might cause you to stop or doubt what you're doing.

- Who might be helpful to you in implementing your plan? Who else?

- What might be the best timing to move forward?

- What might be a difficult time to move forward?

- What resources do I need to have in place?

- Which people can I go to for support?

- What attitudes do I need to work on or to let go?

- What can I do to turn a tough day around?

EXECUTING YOUR PLAN Phase 2: Formulating a Plan-Convergent:

Modify your solution statements; select and organize action steps.

The list of possible action steps will now be condensed and organized into a workable plan. This process details a common, time-tested method for organizing a multistep project. The complexity of the solution may require additional project management tools and skills.

Converge: If necessary, modify your solution statement to include any changes you need to make after considering how you will address your key sources of assistance and resistance.

Then form the list of action steps you generated in the divergent phase; mark ones that must be included. Combine, separate, and eliminate where needed. Then organize the steps into a plan by completing a chart. Be sure to include immediate, short intermediate and long-term actions and to define those terms. For example, does immediate mean 24 hours, 48 hours? Is the short term 3 months? 6 months?

Just because you have a solution doesn't mean it'll be executed at your speed.

Mindset piece

This is you putting your plan into action; that is, taking it from the drawing board to reality in the world. To do this, you need to coax it to life, set the time aside you need, show others what you are doing, and navigate your path.

Two important factors emerge to manage this process.

1) Accountability to take action. Doing the activities you need to do to get where you want to go is paramount. You may elect to hire a coach or an assistant.

2) Mindset. Managing your mindset during the process is just as important as the actual footwork. There is a term in the Creativity World called Tolerance for Ambiguity. It

refers to the in-between time when a solution is not quite formed but is being worked on. There may not be a light at the end of the tunnel, there may be many unanticipated changes, and timelines may not be what was expected. How you manage yourself mentally while this is going on is everything.

Managing your mindset during the unknown is required throughout the creative process. Once you are actually making changes in the real world, there will be times when it feels like you don't know what is going on. You may feel like nothing is happening or that you have made a big mistake. You may think it is not unfolding in your timeframe.

Tolerating ambiguity is part of the process of navigating change and bringing something new to life. Remember that when doubt, fear, or exhaustion rears its head.

Think of those moments as the middle school of the creative process. During middle school, you're in the middle– you're not a little kid anymore but you're not in high school either. You feel awkward, un-cool, and uncertain, and you think you know it all, but your perspective is limited.

However, if you show up 5 days a week and attempt to learn what is in front of you and do your work, you get through it. It's just like diving into a lake and trying to swim to the opposite shore. At some point you're equally distant from either side. You're sure to feel a little uncomfortable and scared and your head might start telling you all sorts of stories, but what will you do? Turn around and go back, or tell your head "Thanks for sharing" and keep going?

The point, is there will be moments, even days, where

you feel stuck, stuck, stuck. When that happens, I remind my clients to imagine that the project is just incubating. Continue to do your part.

Maybe you need to busy yourself in another area for the moment while this piece over here sorts itself out. Sometimes you just need to take a diversion instead and during that diversion you unexpectedly uncover the thing that brings it all together or helps you take the next step.

Now that you know it won't be a straight line that happens on your time, are you ready to proceed?

Part 3:

Taking Action for Real-World Change

Chapter 13:

Where Are You Now?

What you gained

You have now completed one round of the Creative CORE process. Congratulations! Take a moment to reflect, consider what you have learned, and pat yourself on the back for sticking with it.

I hope your experience with The Creative CORE helped you see the ramifications creative thinking can have throughout your life. No longer can you say you are not creative, because now you understand the mechanics of creativity and how to use them intentionally.

You know that there are steps, phases, mindsets, and tools that can be applied to any situation where you have identified a problem, a question or a vision, and there is no ready-made path to get there.

You hold the key to your own liberation and expression, because you have a resource that can help drive your life forward. You can use the process with yourself, or as a guide for others who feel stuck in their lives.

You may find it a relief to be able to assist others, not by feeling that you have to solve their problems for them but rather by using the framework and holding space for them to consider how to navigate their own options.

Did you notice the power of asking open-ended questions? Could you see how these types of questions naturally form while using the statement starters?

Open-ended questions engage the mind by causing trains of thought that get ideas flowing. When you use these types of questions with others, you are encouraging their own ability to generate ideas and see possible solutions.

Taking it one step further, you can help them think through the strengths and weaknesses of their ideas. That type of interaction boosts critical thinking, as well as resiliency. If you can help someone look objectively at their own idea and discern what is good vs what could use improvement, they can save time and develop a thicker skin. This translates into being able to receive feedback as part of a process, rather than a condemnation or negation of their creative abilities. It is part of learning to appreciate and participate in a dynamic creative process.

Reflections on process: what is different now?

Thinking back on your original situation, what new thoughts or insights do you have about the situation that are different?

How do you see yourself differently in relation to the situation?

In what ways was it helpful to follow this process of applying creative thinking?

What did you discover about the way you perceived your challenge? Did it change after you ran it through this process?

How was this approach different from what you may have done in the past?

What possibility do you see available to you now that you have this experience under your belt?

What did you like most about the process?

Did some aspects feel more natural? Were any challenging?

Can you think of ways or people you could include to support you in the future?

Creativity and self-empowerment

Flexible thinking makes you more valuable. With the ability to think creatively you have the capacity to expand your influence and become a multi-purpose contributor to any environment. Now that you understand that using your creativity does not necessarily mean you have to be an artist, you are able to consider the practical implications and the improvements you can bring to your life.

Far from being something that is whimsical, creativity makes you more valuable.

At work you can be tasked to solve bigger problems, step up as a leader, and contribute in new ways. If you are navigating change in your life, you can task yourself with thinking bigger, considering riskier choices, and stretching yourself into new arenas.

By habituating yourself to apply these thinking skills, you become more than a cog in a wheel, you become a person with an ability to contribute by infusing your own spirit of originality. This can help keep yourself engaged and entertained.

You have learned that embracing the ambiguity inherent in the change process is a key skill to moving forward. When you notice that ambiguity, it is a signal that you are in the midst of the creative process. The end is not quite in sight yet. There may be loose ends that need to come together. Just because you are experiencing this does not mean that nothing is happening or that you should stop and retreat.

Research shows deathbed regrets are not about money and security. What do you want to look back on?

In 2012 a palliative care nurse named Bronnie Ware wrote a book about the regrets of the dying. She discovered that the number one regret was "I wish I'd had the courage to live a life true to myself, not the life others expected of me." Other regrets had to do with how they spent their time, made connections, shared their feelings or made friends. The author was surprised that the regrets were not about money and security, as that is what we spend so much time focused on generating.

When you project forward and imagine yourself waking up one day and knowing that there is no more time left, is there anything you would regret if you had taken no action to experience it?

Could that motivate you now? Do you need a little creative thinking to figure out how to do or experience the thing/s?

Take a moment and write some notes about what it is now so you can remind yourself

_____

_____

_____

Which section did you like best?

Different people have different preferences within the process. The Creative CORE pieces are each a bit different and different people have different preferences for the pieces. Some people love to generate ideas and can give you a long list before you have 5. Others love to take a plan and just get moving, while others ponder and like to develop the plan before taking it into action. Think about your favorite part; do you notice whether you tend to do that kind of thinking in general?

If you're someone who loves to see the big picture, build a team that can help you parse out the steps in a plan or can help you be accountable to the plan you want to execute. There's no shame in being a dreamer, but it is a shame if your dreams never take shape because that's just not your wheelhouse.

If you'd like to dive more deeply into this topic, there is an assessment called *Foursight* to learn more about your own preference or that of team or family members you work with. (www.foursightonline.com)

Now that you are an adult who has flourished somewhere in the world, you can give yourself permission to re-evaluate from the perspective of creative satisfaction and adjust your trajectory in a responsible manner.

For the purposes of teaching the process, we must conclude here. In the confinements of a book, I can't direct your action plan. I can only offer you tools and resources that will help you implement them. Depending on the scope of your plan, there may be many stakeholders or just you in charge.

Whichever the case may be, you will likely need accountability buddies, people to be your cheerleaders and ones who will check in on your progress. The exciting thing about a creative solution is that it breathes new life into a dull, stuck, intractable situation. Take action quickly so that you can use the momentum you have created to start turning your desire into active change. You don't want to get stuck in the momentary high of a good idea.

Allow your truth and desire to be simple so that fewer pieces have to line up for you to experience satisfaction. Complication is usually ego driven, and ego can really mess things up. It's the reason people say honesty is the best policy; truth is uncomplicated once you dig.

If you did this work, rest assured you are in process and you are going somewhere. Allow yourself to be surprised and remember to embrace the ambiguity.

You will likely have to modify and adjust and continue to use your divergent and convergent skills. If you find yourself on a path that doesn't feel like it's the right one, review your Vision work. If you are on a good road but stuck, you might need to generate some ideas.

Once you have the skills and understand that there are phases to the process that repeat, you can intentionally use the tools to ask the right questions that will help you generate new plans, ideas, or solutions. However, enacting your plan is where the rubber meets the road. If you have big plans that take you into uncharted territories and you need help from people you have yet to meet, you will need to use your creative muscles all the time to create the opportunities and openings you need. Life can be an adventure, and your creative wiles can open the doors to possibilities and opportunities you have dreamed of.

Happy creating.

Please share examples of stories or your work in the Facebook group at https://www.facebook.com/groups/creativecorebook

We have a lively community of creative thinking people who even help each other brainstorm and share how they have navigated to new solutions.

Chapter 14:

Beyond the Book

Even if you're a highly motivated person, staying committed to a process can wear you thin.

Patience and confidence will get tested, doubts will creep in, and excuses can start to take priority.

You can protect yourself from these occurrences by planning ahead and buying yourself an extra layer of support, encouragement, and accountability.

This can take the form of personal coaching or membership in a mastermind group. Both tools are effective ways to mitigate this natural phenomenon and keep you moving forward.

Coaching is great if you like the focus on you, want one-on-one support, or just like to keep your process a bit more private.

I am here to help you feel seen and heard, to keep you going and, wherever possible, to break through mental and emotional blocks. These blocks may look like impostor syndrome, heavy resistance, excuse making, self-doubt, and fatigue.

A mastermind is a good choice if you're working in new

territory or want extra support with strategy and execution. The mastermind group becomes like an extended brain, all thinking on behalf of your situations. It's a place to contribute to others with your knowledge, and to receive their knowledge.

If you have liked what I have presented and gotten the sense of my voice and spirit, perhaps you'd like to work with me directly. I offer coaching, masterminds and workshops.

Vivian's offerings

My passion is creating environments that allow people to use their creativity as a tool and thereby change their lives for the better.

My classes support both personal growth and professional development. Your CORE skills transfer to both arenas and the focus of the emphasis can be changed depending on where you wish to see growth.

The main outcomes of my work are:
- Becoming a more creative thinker
- Navigating change gracefully
- Feeling more confident
- A revitalized sense of purpose
- Rediscovering fun
- Improved confidence
- Improved communication
- Courage to move towards a vision

Chapter 18:

Parting Thoughts

As you approach change and stretch out of your safety zone into new experiences, are you going to let the shadow cause you to turn around and run away, or will you remember to recognize it for what it is: a projection, a trick of the environment that has no actual ability to hurt you.

Happy creating.

Stay focused on your goals and enjoy the process.

To contact me, please email
vivian@creativitymuse.com
to ask for a discovery call.

You can learn more about expanding your creativity or download worksheets at
https://creativitymuse.com

Acknowledgements

To all my creative problem solvers known and unknown, with immense gratitude and respect for showing me the wisdom of the creative spirit and what it means to be a flexible thinker.

To all the coaches who helped me: Al Watt, Ashley Mansour and Steph Ritz. Your guidance were the stepping stones along the path as I worked through the C.O.R.E. myself. Steph, your patience in getting me through the finish line is truly appreciated. Ashley you got me through the first draft, and Al you got me the direction.

To the Wizards of Osborn the "WOO's" my graduate school cohort, I appreciate you all and the journey we took together learning about creativity and each putting our own spin on this natural cycle of creativity.

To my friends and family, thanks for believing in me, showing up for my classes and workshops and encouraging me in this process.

Metaphor
by Vivian Geffen

While in the ocean today I saw fish swimming all around me. The movement startled me but I was pleased to realize the water was so clear. I was there doing my usual swimming and meditating. I continued swimming towards my goal, which is a buoy.

The farther out I went, the murkier the water became. At some point I noticed something large and dark swimming beneath me. It looked ominous and I became unsettled. My heart began to pound and I started to swim faster to put distance between me and it.

I couldn't tell what it was. Was it a stingray? A school of fish? A tiger shark?

It wasn't leaving me alone. I got panicky and decided to turn around and go back to shore. With my eyes closed and head down, I swam as fast as I could in the direction of safety. Eventually I reached a point where the water was still deep, but no longer murky.

The darkness was still following me; how could this be? Having enough of this weirdness I decided to be brave, so I stopped and stared down at whatever was in the water.

What I saw was that it was my shadow, cast through the water onto the sea floor below me! I had been trying to outswim my shadow.

What a relief! I had to chuckle and then thought, "What a great metaphor for how something harmless can stop you dead in your tracks and halt your growth."

www.ingramcontent.com/pod-product-compliance
Lightning Source LLC
LaVergne TN
LVHW051246080426
835513LV00016B/1774